D0273490

THE WRONG MAN

The Shooting of
STEVEN WALDORF
and the Hunt for
DAVID MARTIN

DICK KIRBY

The
History
Press

This book is dedicated to Len and Beryl Monica Waldorf,
who displayed great courage, dignity and compassion
throughout this case.

And also to Ann, who, like the Waldorf family, waited,
wondered and worried.

First published 2016

The History Press
The Mill, Brimscombe Port
Stroud, Gloucestershire, GL5 2QG
www.thehistorypress.co.uk

British Library Cataloguing in Publication Data.
A catalogue record for this book is available from the British Library.

ISBN 978 0 7509 6413 5

Typesetting and origination by The History Press
Printed in Great Britain

Also by the Author

Contents

Acknowledgements

I should like to thank first my long-time chum, the intrepid reporter Jeff Edwards for such a splendid foreword. Next Mark Beynon, the commissioning editor at The History Press, for his enthusiasm regarding this book. In addition, Paul Bickley of the Crime Museum, New Scotland Yard; Shannon Stroud, Freedom of Information Advisor, New Scotland Yard; Bob Fenton QGM, Honorary Secretary to the Ex-CID Officers' Association; and Susi Rogol, Editor of the *London Police Pensioner* magazine, all assisted and I am most grateful to them.

Once more, I have to thank my daughter Suzanne Cowper and her husband Steve, together with my daughter Barbara's husband, Rich Jerreat, who successfully guided me through the baffling minefield of computer land.

The following includes those who went to a great deal of trouble for me, some of whom delved into memories which must have been very traumatic, who gave most generously of their time and I am indebted to them. They appear in alphabetical order: Dave Allen, Frederick Arnold, Terry Babbidge QPM, Brian Baister QPM, MA, Roger Baldry, John Barnie, Jim Barrow, the late Nicky Benwell QPM, Alan Berriman, Colin Black, Alan Branch, Linda Brown, Colonel Markham Bryant MBE, DL, Nick Carr, Roger Clements, 'Steve Collins', Michael Conner, Bob Cook, Suzanne Cowper, Clive Cox, Paul Cox, Leo Daniels QPM, Robert Darby, John Devine, Neil Dickens QPM, Ken Dungate, James Finch, Peter Finch, Steve Fletcher, Jim Francis, the late Tony Freeman,

Gerry Gallagher, Mick Geraghty, Martin Gosling MBE, Len Gunn, Gordon Harrison, Colin Hockaday, Steve Holloway, John Jardine, Barbara Jerreat, Len Jessup, Mark Kirby, Gus MacKenzie CFE, ACFS, Bill Miller, Alan Moss, Morgan O'Grady, Martin Power, Lester Purdy, Tom Renshaw, Eddie Roach, Michael Bradley Taylor QPM, John Twomey and Tony Yeoman. My thanks for the use of the photographs goes to Linda Brown, Nick Carr, Peter Finch, Gerry Gallagher, Damian Hinojosa, John Jardine, Len Jessup, Alan Moss, the Metropolitan Police, Lester Purdy, Tom Renshaw, Martin and Maria Steward and the author's collection. Every effort has been made to trace copyright holders and the publishers and I apologise for any inadvertent omissions.

There were others who for a number of reasons either wished to remain anonymous or who were in a position to provide pertinent information and who chose not to do so. Bereft of their assistance, I have endeavoured to ensure that the content of this book is as accurate as possible and acknowledge that any faults or imperfections are mine alone.

As always, I pay tribute to my family for their never-ending love and support; in already mentioning my daughters and their spouses, I naturally include my grandchildren Emma, Jessica and Harry Cowper and Samuel and Annie Grace Jerreat, as well as my sons, Mark and Robert.

Most of all, I salute my wife Ann, who, for over fifty years, has been my dear, loving companion.

Foreword
by Jeff Edwards

Former Chief Crime Correspondent, Daily Mirror, *President of the Crime Reporters' Association*

There is no doubt in my mind that Dick Kirby is the all-time best, most successful, and prolific author of 'real life' books about the British police.

I like to think that, in a very small way, I helped him on that path.

I first met Dick in 1970. He had just been made a fully fledged detective constable posted to the CID (Criminal Investigation Department) at Forest Gate in East London, and I was a fluffy-faced aspiring 21-year-old crime reporter on the local *Newham Recorder*. In those days, unlike the situation now, reporters on local papers could get to meet police officers working at busy London police stations easily and without much restriction. Providing you were considered (in CID parlance) 'a good cock', who would happily stand his round in the pub and knew how to play by the rules, you were usually welcome.

I instinctively liked most of the cops I met back then. Many of them were outgoing, animated, even flamboyant characters, and I enjoyed their endless stories of life at the sharp end on the mean streets of London. I also liked their bonhomie and sense of comradeship, and their slightly jaundiced and sceptical view of life. Perhaps most of all I liked the dark dry humour and the ready wit many of them possessed.

Newham had one of the highest crime rates in the country at the time and the police were always full of stories. Some of these tales were in the best traditions of Dick Barton or Fabian of the Yard. Sometimes the tales were astonishing and full of daring and courage. Some of them were about skill or cunning where good triumphed over evil. Some of them, to be frank, were where a more acceptable sort of evil triumphed over a worse form. Some of the tales were very tall indeed – and some were unprintable in a family newspaper. Grey areas abounded. I had the time of my life!

I can't remember exactly where or how I was introduced to Dick Kirby, except that he was one of those whose blend of fierce hatred of criminals, his disdain of weak and ineffectual senior officers and his loathing of devious lawyers and feeble magistrates made him stand out. With a liking for the cut and thrust of lively debate, a sharp wit and pithy observations on life in general, he was never short of an audience. He was a natural-born storyteller. We hit it off and in many ways our careers ran parallel, him moving up to some of the top crime-fighting units at Scotland Yard, while I went on to a long career as a Fleet Street crime hack.

So how do I claim to have helped give a push to Dick's later career as an author?

In the 1970s almost every police officer I knew was enthralled by the writings of the American author Joseph Wambaugh, who had for many years been a Los Angeles policeman until he turned his hand to writing. What cops everywhere loved about him was his ability to tell it like it really was. On the one hand, it was through compelling documentary stories like *The Onion Field*, where he drew on first-hand experience of terrible events which affected the lives of close colleagues. On the other, he wrote the candidly observed and extremely funny novel *The Choirboys*. Wambaugh was the real deal. He knew exactly how street cops thought, spoke, and acted, because he was one of them. In a way, he was their collective voice.

Dick Kirby was one of his greatest fans.

In 1979, as a crime reporter on the London *Evening News*, I received a phone call from a woman I knew who was working as a publicist for a film company. Hollywood had made a film version of *The Onion Field* which was to be released soon in Britain. As part of the promotion, Joe Wambaugh was coming to London. While he was here he'd expressed a wish to meet some London police officers. Could I be of any assistance? You bet I could.

The choice was easy. I rang Dick and our mutual chum Peter Connor, another East London police detective, and a dinner meeting was arranged. Needless to say, Dick and Joe and Pete got on famously. And following that meeting I know Dick went on to forge a strong friendship with Joe, which endures to this day.

I have no doubt that Dick was inspired by his American counterpart to take up a second career as a writer when he retired from policing. Although their experiences were separated by the width of an entire continent and an ocean, in my opinion there is something similar in the way Joe and Dick write. You could call it shared experience, but it is more than that.

I believe it is because Dick also has the instinctive ability to translate and describe the subtle nuances in the way real police detectives, real cops on the beat working at the sharp end of law enforcement, think, speak, reason and behave.

The story of David Martin and his crimes is an extraordinary one, which Dick tells here in well-researched detail. Crime reporters, sometimes with tongue in cheek, have often used the phrase 'master criminal' to describe well-known villains. I would not call Martin one of those. He was first and foremost dangerous, volatile, ruthless and narcissistic. However, he was, as this book describes, in many ways exceptionally clever and quick of mind. For the police he was a resourceful, determined and formidable foe. In a strange twist, which this book chronicles closely, Martin became as well known perhaps not for what happened to him, but what happened to someone the police thought was him.

The entirely innocent Stephen Waldorf had the misfortune to strongly resemble Martin in appearance. Thus fate conspired to put him in the passenger seat of a car which was being followed through London by an undercover police unit who were looking for David Martin. Because Martin had previously shot and nearly killed a policeman, these officers were psychologically wound as tight as watch springs. Eventually the car, hemmed in by stationary traffic, was riddled with police bullets. Waldorf himself was hit five times and then his skull was fractured with the butt of a detective's pistol. Astonishingly perhaps, he survived and made a full recovery.

Dick Kirby deals with this seminal moment in modern police history with great even-handedness. His description of the surveillance operation which police thought was targeted on David Martin brilliantly conveys the heart-stopping uncertainty, contradictions and chaos that can occur when even the best constructed plans suddenly run out of control. The reason his account is so compelling is because, once again, Dick demonstrates this sixth-sense knowledge of the way genuine police officers reason and react at times of great tension and stress. Like Joe Wambaugh, Dick Kirby is the real deal. He writes with the insight of someone who can only do so when they've lived it and felt it emotionally.

The Waldorf shooting was a watershed for the way British police train and deploy firearms specialists. But as any military man will tell you, few battle plans survive first contact with the enemy, and so it is with the police. If you place deadly force in the hands of anyone, be it well-trained police or ruthless criminals, and add tension and emotion into the mix, it will always be the case that sometimes things will end in catastrophe.

Dick Kirby was a first-class copper and is now a first-class author. Long may he write.

Prologue

I leant back in the rather rickety captain's chair and gazed around at the shabby surroundings in Harry's office, from which he ran his scrap-metal business in Hammersmith, until my eyes finally settled on Harry, sitting behind the desk that separated us.

'I'll always remember turning over a scrappie's yard when I was an aid to CID,' I said reminiscently. 'D'you what he said to me, Harry?'

Harry obligingly raised his eyebrows, exhibiting a polite modicum of interest.

'He said, "Let's face it, Guv – ninety per cent of the gear in here is bent and the other ten per cent's iffy."'

Harry gave a blackened, gap-toothed grin. 'I hope your first-class gave you a bollocking for going there in the first place,' he replied.

The 'first-class' that Harry was referring to was the station's detective sergeant (first class) who was traditionally in charge of the aids to CID; and it was alleged that some of the first-classes offered a degree of protection to the scrappies in return for a highly unofficial bursary, to save them from the depredations of the feral aids who, it was said, would nick anybody for anything.

But I was able to smile at Harry in spite of the implied insult and I shook my head. 'Not on that occasion,' I replied. 'Because the first-class was with me and I'll tell you something else, Harry.' I leaned forward and picked up a rather wide, but weightless, spring-back binder which should have housed Harry's legitimate business transactions. 'It's amazing what you can find if you're prepared to look for it,' and with that I dropped it on the table. A thin coating of dust arose from the binder, a mute testimony that little had been added to the file for some time. I added, 'Or not, as the case may be.'

Harry's jowly, lugubrious features sagged and he swallowed noisily. 'Am I going to be turned over, Guv?' he asked plaintively. 'Are you putting it on me?'

Abruptly, I stood up. 'I really don't fancy looking round the place – not right now, that is,' I replied. 'Tell you what – why don't you and I go and have a drink, and I'll tell you what I've got in mind.'

Harry brightened up immediately. 'Right!' he said and off we went to the pub round the corner. I felt fairly sure that Harry had something I wanted and that 'something' was the whereabouts of Eric.

This was a classic case of 'the stick and the carrot'. The stick was the implied threat that if that scrap metal yard was to be searched – as Harry had said, 'turned over' – then it was quite probable that some non-ferrous metal of an incriminating nature would be found, which Harry would find perplexing to explain away. Given the paucity of invoices in his spring-back binder, Harry might have had to have accepted, with ill grace, the inevitability of 'a stretch' – or, to the uninitiated, twelve months' imprisonment. But then, almost immediately, I had offered him the far more acceptable compromise of a carrot: the offer of a drink in more salubrious surroundings than his odoriferous office and where Harry could marshal all of his perspicacity to determine precisely what was on offer.

By today's standards, you may think that this was slightly unconventional policing but this is now and that was on Friday 14 January 1983. Unorthodox or not, that was the way things got done during those halcyon days with New Scotland Yard's Flying Squad – commonly known as 'The Sweeney' and more officially as C8 Department – and now I'll tell you how I came to be in Harry's scrap yard.

Over the previous two months, my Flying Squad team and I had effected the arrest of the leader of a highly organised and deeply despicable gang of blaggers – robbers, to you. They had carried out raids on the homes of elderly, wealthy women in the Belgravia area of London and attacked, chloroformed and bound and gagged them before making off with their treasured possessions. Two such raids had resulted in the gang becoming £30,000 richer. Men who make their living by attacking elderly ladies seldom possess much moral fibre and the gang leader was no exception to the rule. I had arrested him, with the aid of that very large officer from Ulster, Gerry Gallagher – of whom you'll hear much more later – at a quarter-to-two in the morning as he endeavoured to make an escape through the window of a first-floor flat in West London. Not only did the gang leader confess to everything he'd done, he also informed us of robberies that he and his gang had planned to carry out in the future, took us to the venues of these planned robberies and identified each of the other gang members. They were brought in, admitted their respective parts in the individual offences, were charged and were now in prison, on remand.

And to be fair – this is no time for false modesty – it was a terrific case, one in a long line of sensational arrests involving snouts, fast drives across London and punch-ups with seasoned villains. So in this current investigation, everybody was accounted for – everybody, that is, but Eric. We knew *who* he was but not *where* he was. Eric, whose criminal career had commenced over twenty years previously, was no fool. He was constantly on the move and if the gang leader had possessed an idea as to his whereabouts, I have no doubt he'd have told us. But he didn't, so he couldn't. Therefore, I put the word about and then I got the whisper that if anybody knew of Eric's address, it'd be Harry the Scrappie.

So that was how Harry and I came to be drinking large scotches on that cold January evening; and it paid off. The address he gave me for Eric was way out in the boondocks and as I bade farewell to Harry, I also made it quite clear that if Eric should receive a warning telephone call of our impending arrival, our next meeting would be not quite so convivial.

In the ordinary run of things, I should have submitted Harry's name, under a suitable nom de plume, to be considered for an ex-gratia payment from the Yard's informants' fund for his valuable input into revealing the whereabouts of a much-wanted blagger, who in the due process of time would share among his contemporaries a total of twenty-six years' imprisonment. Not on this occasion, though. Harry had profited from not having his business brought under careful scrutiny; it was a case of quid pro quo.

It had gone six o'clock when I made my way back to the Flying Squad car, a nondescript Rover 3500, parked some distance away; my driver, Tony Freeman, was behind the wheel. All squad vehicles were fitted with two-tone sirens, a gong and two radios: the main set could send and receive messages to and from Information Room at Scotland Yard and vehicles all over the Metropolitan Police District (MPD). There was a second, small set, also known as the 'car-to-car-radio' and these were used during squad (and other specialist units) operations for contact between the operational vehicles but which only had a limited transmitting and receiving range – about two to three miles. Usually, since the vehicles were inevitably in close proximity to one another, that did not present a problem. As I got into the car, I asked, 'Anything happening on the air?'

Tony shook his head. 'A right load of that CB[1] crap on the main set,' he replied, and then he added, 'Funny thing, Dick. I think C11 must be nearby. I heard them on the small set a little while ago – all of a sudden, I heard someone say, "Oh, fuck!" Dunno what it was all about.'

---

1. Citizens' Band radio, a mercifully short-lived fad whereby amateur radio enthusiasts searched the airways to speak consummate gibberish to complete strangers.

'Nothing else since then?' I asked and Tony shook his head. 'Right, let's head back to CO,[2] see if anything's happening.'

Tony dropped me off on Scotland Yard's concourse and I got into the lift and ascended to the fourth floor, Victoria Block, pushed open the swing doors, turned left and walked down to the end of the long corridor (Flying Squad offices on the left and C11 – or Criminal Intelligence – on the right) towards the main squad office. There was no one about; it seemed that they'd heeded the wise police dictum: that it was POETS[3] day.

There was just one person in the squad office: Jim Moon, once an ace squad driver, now in retirement supplementing his pension by manning the telephones and the radio.

'Anything happening, Jim?' I asked but Jim shook his head. 'Nothing for you, Sargie.'

I picked up the Police Almanac which housed the telephone numbers for all the police stations in all the United Kingdom's different constabularies, found the one covering the area where Eric was living and asked the local detective inspector to nab him for us. 'That's great!' responded the Inspector. 'We want the little bugger as well, but we didn't know where he was!' Of course, the Inspector hadn't made the acquaintance of 'Harry the Scrappie'.

I booked off duty and went home to Upminster, Essex, rescued a steak pie from the oven, which, had I arrived home three hours previously when it had been freshly cooked, would have been quite tasty, made incisions into it to release the scorching heat and poured myself a glass of red. As I finished the meal, I poured myself another glass and then I realised it was time for the news. I switched the television on. There on the screen was a yellow Mini, registration number GYF 117W, its doors wide open, spotlights

---

2. Commissioner's Office, New Scotland Yard.
3. Piss Off Early, Tomorrow's Saturday.

illuminating it and the commentator was saying, 'A man has been critically injured in a police ambush in a West London street in what may be a case of mistaken identity. Witnesses said marksmen surrounded a car in a traffic jam in Pembroke Road in Earls Court and opened fire.'

Just then my wife Ann came into the room. 'Is this what made you late?'

I shook my head. 'No, first I've heard about it … shh … I want to hear …'

'The driver was shot several times in the head and body,' continued the commentator. 'Scotland Yard said the ambush was part of an operation to recapture escaped prisoner David Martin.' Now the camera focused on one of the first witnesses on the scene, secretary Jane Lamprill, who said the man seemed very badly injured. 'He was about thirty,' she said, 'but I couldn't even see the colour of his hair because of the blood.'

'Christ!' I exclaimed. 'The wrong bloody man!'

'No, they said it wasn't clear if it was this Martin man or not,' said Ann, but just then the phone rang. It was the Inspector from the constabulary to say that Eric had been arrested. 'He's singing like a bird to our job,' he chuckled, 'although he did look a bit worried when I said the squad wanted to have a word with him!'

'He fucking needs to be!' I scoffed. 'Just lock him up tonight and we'll be along to see him tomorrow morning.' I rang off and telephoned the rest of the team for an early start the following day. As I went up to bed, the name 'David Martin' was going round and round in my head. Who was he? All right, it was a fairly common name but where the hell had I heard it before?

The next day, Saturday, Tony and I, together with the rest of my team were heading north out of London. We reached our destination, a small market town in the middle of nowhere, where I met, and spoke fairly briskly to Eric who promptly confessed everything confessable in a written statement. The constabulary officers wanted to charge him with their offence, take him before the local Magistrates' Court and remand him in custody and this suited me to the ground. Later, we could have him produced on a Home Office order to join the rest of the gang on a remand hearing at our Magistrates' Court and then we could commit the whole lot of them to the Old Bailey for trial.

We set off back to London and I was glad that the 'Eric' business had been transacted so quickly. Today was my mother's 78th birthday and since my father had died four months earlier, it was especially important for me and the family to be with her at this time.

As we reached the borders of the Metropolitan Police District, I called up the Flying Squad office on the RT set: 'Central 899 from Central 954; Jim, book us back in the MPD, please – see you soon.'

The reply was immediate: 'Central 954 from Central 899; get over to 'Delta Delta' as quick as you can – there's a flap on!'

I acknowledged the call as we came out of the Hanger Lane gyratory system and on to the A40. 'Delta Delta' – otherwise Paddington Green police station and 'D' Division's Divisional Headquarters – was just a short distance away; and as we tore towards the A40(M), two-tones wailing, I was thinking, 'Why Paddington? Why us?'

All was soon revealed. The nick was crowded with police officers, a lot of them Flying Squad. It was from 'D' Division that the operation had originated to hunt down David Martin, who, charged with shooting a police constable, had escaped from custody. Somehow – nobody seemed quite sure how –

matters had gone tragically wrong and had resulted in armed police shooting and seriously wounding an innocent young man, a 26-year-old film editor named Steven Waldorf. One of the officers who had fired shots which had injured Waldorf was attached to 'D' Division.

Morale at Paddington Green police station was, quite understandably, at rock bottom and the operation, which had been headed by 'D' Division's Detective Superintendent George Ness, was now, on orders from on high, being handed over to Commander Frank Cater who the previous week had taken over the running of the Flying Squad.

My team and I were part of 12 Squad, which along with 10 Squad was now appointed to the investigation. The officer in charge of operational matters was Detective Chief Superintendent Don Brown, who I later discovered was a seasoned and highly respected squad officer. Arriving on the same day as Frank Cater, Brown had returned to the Flying Squad for his third and final tour.

I didn't know Don Brown but I knew Frank Cater; he'd been my boss when I'd served on the Serious Crime Squad and as the meeting broke up he murmured to me, 'We need to wind this up as soon as possible, Dick.' I nodded and replied absently, 'Right, Guv,' but my mind was on other matters – from the photographs and the background I'd seen and heard of the target, I'd just realised where I knew Martin's name from. The Flying Squad hunt for David Martin was beginning right now, but my private war with Martin had started ten years previously.

Note: The correct spelling of Steven Waldorf's name is with a 'v' despite many online resources and newspapers spelling it with 'ph'.

First Sightings

Before I progress any further with the story of both the shooting of an innocent man and the hunt for a man who was anything but innocent, I have to introduce you to the police world of many years ago and of which I was a member.

In the early 1970s, I was appointed a detective constable of the Metropolitan Police and was posted to Forest Gate police station in the East End of London, reputedly the busiest sectional station in the Metropolitan Police. I couldn't have been happier. I'd had a successful career as an aid to CID, plus I'd scored high marks at the ten-week Initial (Junior) Course at the Detective Training School. In addition, I'd achieved the highest number of arrests on 'K' Division and now, having successfully passed two stiff selection boards, as a fully fledged member of the Criminal Investigation Department I needed to make my bones as a detective. The whole area (it was colloquially referred to as 'The Manor') – Forest Gate, Upton Park and Manor Park – was a hotbed of villains and villainy and I simply couldn't wait to get stuck into them.

As an aid to CID, our brief had been to get out and patrol the streets, keep observations, follow, stop and arrest suspects and cultivate informants. Now as a member of the CID proper, I investigated reported crimes and attended the Magistrates' Court practically every day; it was a kind of mini Stock Exchange, filled with the flotsam and jetsam of society, where deals were struck, promises made, informants procured, prisoners remanded and evidence presented. The rest of the time I was attending Crown Courts, meeting informants, typing reports, searching suspect premises and arresting burglars, robbers and fraudsmen. There were simply not enough hours in the day; and at this time the CID were not paid overtime. So much was going on that if I was unable to immediately arrest a local suspect, I'd leave word with their friends and relations for the culprit to surrender at the nick at a specified time, and they usually did.

Right from the start I tore through the underworld like a dervish. I arrested four tearaways wanted for grievous bodily harm, caught one of the last, great cat burglars and his receiver and broke up a highly unpleasant gang of half a dozen blackmailers. A husband-and-wife team were wanted for fraud all over the country; I received a tip that they were about to leave their hotel in the Romford Road and raced down there just in time to stop them in their car, which was loaded with swag. An Arab sheikh in full tribal regalia who was carrying out a fraudulent transaction in a bank was surprised to be seized, addressed as 'cock' and unceremoniously bundled into my car, and when I was attacked by two young thugs whom I'd arrested for possessing offensive weapons, I was restless while on sick leave to return to duty so that I could get out to nick some more. This, as you will imagine, played havoc with my home life. It's a small miracle that Ann and I are still happily married after fifty years.

I reached for the ringing telephone in the CID office on that particular Monday morning; it was the manager of a jeweller's shop in Green Street, to tell me that a man was at the premises attempting to purchase goods by means of a stolen credit card. I slammed the phone down and, shouting at another detective constable to follow me, I raced down the stairs to the station yard where my car, a powerful Ford Corsair 2000 GT, was parked. We roared out of the yard, turned right into Finden Road and almost immediately left into Green Street. 'You'll break our necks, the way you're driving,' sighed my companion, who was not entirely fired with enthusiasm for this investigation, as we tore south along the thoroughfare, paying only lip service to the restrictions imposed by the Road Traffic Act. 'He won't be there,' he insisted. 'As soon as the manager went to phone, he'll have been long gone.'

Privately I too thought that this might be the case but while a possibility of catching a fraudsman red-handed existed, I wanted to give it my best shot. Pulling up outside the jewellers, I ran towards the shop entrance and as I did so, a young man started to leave. There was absolutely nothing about him to attract suspicion; he was extremely smartly dressed in a pinstripe 'company director' style suit, slim, about five feet nine, dark blond hair, a slight tan, aged in his mid-twenties and looked entirely unconcerned as he courteously stepped to one side to let me enter the jewellers. He then began unhurriedly scrutinising the wares in the shop window in the same way that any discerning customer who had yet to make up his mind might do.

I rushed up to the manager. 'Right, where is he?' I demanded and given what was to happen, I now realise that a courteous, more structured approach might have been called for.

The manager raised his eyebrows. 'To whom are you referring?'

'The bloke with the stolen credit card,' I testily replied.

'And you are?' he enquired.

'Police from Forest Gate,' I replied, and I was getting quite irritated because by now, it was obvious that the suspect had departed before our arrival and this was the manager's way of putting me in my place for not getting there sooner.

Nodding thoughtfully, the manager asked, 'Have you any – er – identification?'

I snatched out my warrant card which the manager ostentatiously examined before nodding his approval. 'Right – now was it you I spoke to on the phone at Forest Gate police station about five minutes ago?' I asked. He conceded that this was so.

'And did you tell me there was someone in the shop trying to buy goods with a stolen credit card?' Again, with pursed lips, he nodded in agreement.

'So how long ago was it that he left?' I asked.

The manager languidly waved in the general direction of the door. 'He went out,' he replied, 'just as you came in!'

'You wanker!' I roared, turned and rushed out of the shop, looked left, then right, just in time to see a pair of well-tailored trouser legs disappear round the corner into Plashet Grove.

As I dashed up to the junction, I heard the roar of a powerful car engine starting up. Turning the corner, there facing me was a Jaguar XJ-12 with the fraudsman behind the wheel. As I ran towards the car, I noticed that the car's front passenger window was open, so I plunged in, hoping to grab the ignition key. With that, the driver slammed the car's automatic transmission into 'drive' and drove off fast, with me half-in and half-out of the vehicle.

I said afterwards that I'd be able to recognise him again because of the imprint that my knuckles made on the side of his face, but don't you believe it. As pugilists reading this are aware, to effectively deliver a straight right, you need the transference of power, driving off the ball of the right foot and turning the hip and shoulder in the direction of your opponent. You try it when you're lying horizontally, clinging on to a speeding car with one hand! Yes, I gave him a dig but what with the lack of force of the punch, plus the rush of adrenaline he must have been experiencing, it had little or no effect.

As he reached the junction with Green Street, he braked sharply and I was thrown from the car. I rolled over in the roadway a couple of times and as I got to my feet, I heard the furious sounding of car horns and saw the Jaguar swerving crazily across the junction with Green Street and then swing left into Plashet Road. I dashed across the junction but by the time I got to Plashet Road, the car had vanished. It was only later that I discovered that the Jaguar – which had been reported stolen from the Paddington area – had been abandoned in Lucas Avenue, the fourth turning on the left. It was thought that the driver – who had discarded his jacket, to prevent recognition – might have escaped by turning left out of Lucas Avenue into Harold Road and thence the short distance into Upton Park Underground station.

I was furious – furious with the manager of the shop, furious with the fraudsman who could have caused me serious injury and furious with myself for failing to arrest him, by not being quicker off the mark. Matters were not improved when I limped back to the police station where, with a commendable lack of tact and concern for my well-being, the first-class sergeant scoffed, 'Huh! Couldn't catch a bleedin' cold!' Doc Lazarus MBE, the Divisional Surgeon (who would later say that he thought that I was his best customer), tut-tutted as he examined my lumps and bumps from being thrown off the car, diagnosed strained chest muscles from hanging on to it, prescribed paracetamol and told me to 'get on with it'.

So I did. Simmering quietly, I put the details in the crime book, circulated details of the fraudsman and the details of the card he'd been using and cracked on with a fresh inquiry.

Months later, I received notification that the fraudsman had been arrested somewhere else in London and had been charged with a whole series of offences; when he appeared at court, he had been sentenced to a long term of imprisonment.

I looked at his name. Martin. David Ralph Martin. Aged 26 and born in Paddington. Never heard of him. And he wasn't a local lad. So how did he know about Lucas Avenue and the close proximity to a secondary getaway route via Upton Park station? Had he taken the trouble to plot an alternative escape, prior to going into the jewellers, just in case he got tumbled? And what was more, I couldn't get out of my mind the slick way in which he'd strolled out of the shop; that took a lot of nerve.

Then I shrugged my shoulders and forgot about him.

I might have thought that I was cock-o'-the-walk in the CID office at Forest Gate but I still had a lot to learn about criminal behaviour and psychology in general, and crooks like Martin in particular. Slick? Christ, I didn't know the meaning of the word.

Fraudsman

From undistinguished beginnings, David Martin's life can only be described as extraordinary. He was born in Paddington on 25 February 1947 and was brought up in a council flat in Finsbury Park, the only child to Ralph and Joan Martin. For all of his life and whatever he did, right or wrong, his father defended, made excuses for and idolised him. Father and son had a common predisposition: both of them hated the police.

In common with the majority of law-breakers, Martin's criminal career commenced during his formative years. He first appeared at North London Juvenile Court on 19 April 1963 where, for unauthorised taking of a motor vehicle and associated offences, he was fined a total of £4 and was disqualified from driving for twelve months. Less than three months later he was back at the same court, for stealing petrol from a car. On this occasion, he was fined £5 and his father was bound over in the sum of £15 for twelve months to ensure his son's good behaviour. And it appeared to work. Two years went by and the twelve months, both for Martin's disqualification from driving and his father's recognisance, passed without incident.

But this changed in June 1965 when he appeared at Bow Street Magistrates' Court. For threatening behaviour and assaulting a police officer outside a club 'without realising who he was', as he would later say, he was sentenced to three months in a detention centre.

Martin was not well educated but he was highly intelligent and he had a natural ability to turn his hand to anything electrical or mechanical; following his release from detention in September 1965, he trained as a motor mechanic. It did not last long; within five months he appeared at Highgate Magistrates' Court, where for stealing items from his employer, he was placed on probation for two years. And that was the end of any pretence of honest work for a thoroughly dishonest employee; he ignored the counsel of his probation officer and from then on, Martin would channel his expertise into matters purely criminal, especially stealing cars.

It caught up with him in July 1967 when at the Middlesex Area Sessions, for obtaining property by false pretences, three cases of larceny, two cases of storebreaking and stealing a car – and requesting twenty-one other cases to be taken into consideration – he was sentenced to Borstal Training and disqualified from driving for five years.

During 1968, 1,425 inmates escaped from Borstal; Martin was one of them. He sprang a lock, scaled the boundary wall and was away. It was some time before he was caught and during his unofficial parole, he had been busy. He had taken a car without the owner's consent and that, plus dangerous driving, driving while disqualified and stealing items, including a .22 starting pistol which he put to good use by producing it with intent to resist arrest, resulted in him being returned to Borstal Training when he appeared at the Inner London Quarter Sessions in November 1968. He also asked for a further twelve other offences to be taken into consideration from while he was on the run.

To those unaware of the term, the now redundant Borstal Training was a period of incarceration of between six months to two years awarded to young offenders in the often forlorn hope that they would receive reformative training. Martin was one of that forsaken number; he served the full two years.

As soon as he was released, Martin plunged once more into criminality. Appearing at West London Magistrates' Court, he was committed to the Inner London Quarter Sessions for sentence in December 1969 and, for two cases of obtaining goods by means of a forged instrument, handling stolen goods, theft from a vehicle, unauthorised taking of a vehicle and driving while disqualified, he was sentenced to a total of twenty-one months' imprisonment and disqualified from driving for a further twelve months.

Released on 27 January 1971, that was the last occasion that Martin would plead guilty to anything; in fact, as will be seen, he wouldn't plead not guilty either. His ego was going into orbit. His passionate loathing for those in authority, particularly the police, was developing and in addition, a life-long fascination for locks and security devices began to evolve.

He gathered associates around him and his future criminal enterprises would display enormous cunning and sophistication for a young man, still in his mid-twenties. David Martin was simply going to take on the establishment.

Eddie Roach had joined the Metropolitan Police in 1955. He had worked at St John's Wood, Albany Street and Paddington Green and after a stint with the Metropolitan and City Company Fraud Department, he was promoted to detective sergeant and posted to Hampstead police station where he ran a very successful crime squad.

In September 1972, due to a sudden upsurge in crime in the neighbourhood, the divisional commander of the area covering the wealthy properties in Hampstead, Swiss Cottage and West Hampstead decided to create a crime squad, consisting of ten temporary detective constables (the successors to aids to CID), ten uniform police constables working in plain clothes and a uniform sergeant. Due to Roach's undisputed success of previously running a crime squad on 'E' Division, he was the natural choice to head the squad. The commander gave Roach complete authority in selecting his staff, told Roach to report to him directly and provided an office for the squad at West Hampstead police station, which had just been opened that year at 21 Fortune Green Road, West Hampstead, NW6. Roach would later say, 'Detective work is fifty per cent common sense, forty percent dedication and ten percent luck.' The squad commenced its duties on 25 September 1972 and would demonstrate all those investigative attributes in the months which followed.

About a mile to the south of the police station was Langtry Road, NW8, a cul-de-sac just off the junction with Kilburn High Road and Belsize Road. A few days after the formation of the squad, two officers spotted a red BMW 30 CSI parked outside No. 3 Langtry Road. The model was new; only eight of them had been imported into the United Kingdom from Germany. A check revealed that over a week previously on 18 September, a young man had gone to BMW Concessionaires Ltd in Chiswick High Road and had asked for a test drive. He must have possessed an air of plausibility because the management permitted him to do just that; he was handed a key, drove off and vanished. The credible young man was, of course, David Martin but the officers were not aware of that, nor that he was now residing at 3 Langtry Road. The vehicle, which had been allocated registration number LOY 4K, currently bore false plates.

In fact, this vehicle had already been the subject of a high-speed chase where police vehicles, headed by an ace area car driver, Police Constable Mike McAndrew, had lost the BMW. Given Class I and II police drivers' advanced training at Hendon

Driving School, this hardly seemed possible but the explanation was provided by one of Roach's investigating team. 'He was quite fearless in high-speed motor chases,' Colin Black told me, 'and said during interview that if a police car was coming in the opposite direction, he knew they would move out of the way because they didn't want to get killed; he didn't have any fear of death.'

The vehicle was now kept under observation by the police, after they had surreptitiously deflated one of the tyres to prevent the thief from returning and driving off in it. However, the police were unaware that the thief, from the comfort of 3 Langtry Road, was keeping *them* under observation.

After twenty-four hours, during which time Martin had prudently not approached the BMW, the police brought a low-loader to Langtry Road and conveyed the car to West Hampstead police station where it was placed in a bay beneath the CID office, booked in and the owners informed. What the police did not know was that Martin had followed the low-loader to its destination.

The following afternoon, Roach arrived at the police station at two o'clock and saw that the BMW had gone. He was disappointed because he had hoped for a ride in it and also annoyed because he had wanted to ensure the car had been dusted for fingerprints before it was restored to the owners. He therefore checked with the station officer to see if the vehicle had been fingerprinted before he had handed it back; the station officer replied that he had only just come on duty and that he had not had anything to do with the vehicle. The early-turn station officer was contacted; he too had had nothing to do with restoring the car and perusal of the station's documentation revealed that nobody had signed for it. A deeply embarrassing situation had occurred; the stolen car had been re-stolen and it would take another couple of weeks before this conundrum was solved.

Roach's team was split into pairs and they patrolled in and around the area where the BMW had been parked but it was not until 11 October that their patience was rewarded. It was on that date that two officers saw another BMW, white in colour, parked in the same spot that the red BMW had been. This vehicle was older; it had been the property of a certain Hiroshi Kazato and the car had originally displayed QP 270 on the registration plate. However, since David Martin had stolen it exactly five months previously, those plates had long since been replaced with false ones.

Observation was kept on the car; a little later, two men and a woman emerged from the basement flat at 3 Langtry Road, got into the BMW and drove off. They were Clive Adrian Cyril Green, 19-year-old Janet Marie Norman-Phillips – and David Martin. The car was followed for a short distance but one car is not suitable for tailing purposes and the officers were told to break off the observation before the occupants of the BMW realised they were being followed.

It was a prudent move; surveillance was mounted on the flat at Langtry Road in the belief that since the people responsible for the stolen cars had spent so much time there, it would be that address they would return to. Within an hour, they were proved partially right; Green returned to the flat on foot, let himself in with a key and after half an hour he left, carrying a bag. The officers followed to see if he would meet up with anybody else and when he didn't, they stopped him. The bag contained a briefcase, which in turn revealed stolen chequebooks, credit cards and passports plus a large amount of correspondence – all in different names. Later, the flat was searched and the officers were confronted with an Aladdin's cave of property, all stolen or obtained by fraud. While they were there, the flat was visited by Bruce Wood; when his premises were searched, he was found to be in possession of Post Office books and stamps for forgery and he was charged with theft, handling stolen goods and conspiracy. Another man, Hugh Bestic, was arrested and charged with conspiracy to steal mail and obtaining clothing by means of a forged instrument.

Clearly, Green – who was also found to be in possession of 89 milligrammes of cannabis resin – had some explaining to do and he did. He admitted receiving the stolen property and in addition, admitted attempting to pervert the course of public justice by removing those items from the flat, which would have incriminated Norman-Phillips and Co.

The following evening, Martin and Norman-Phillips broke into a flat at 2–6 Hampstead High Street, NW6 where they were disturbed by the occupant. Norman-Phillips made good her escape, but the flat's occupier hit Martin with a table lamp. During the ensuing struggle, the fight spilled out into the street where a passer-by helped restrain Martin. He was taken back into the flat and the police were called. Martin once more tried to escape and was bound with ties and belts until the police arrived.

Upon being interviewed by Roach, it was established that Martin was the second man who had been seen leaving Langtry Road and he admitted stealing the red BMW, then re-stealing it from the police station.

Why had Martin re-stolen the BMW? Was it due to his twisted psyche that he felt that it was 'his' car and that now he was only getting 'his' property back? Possibly. Was it to show off to Norman-Phillips (who had accompanied him), to display his daring and contempt of danger, for her to act as his Boswell, to recount tales of his derring-do to his attentive, albeit small, group of admirers? Again possibly, maybe probably. Or was it to display his absolute contempt for the law? Almost definitely. And why now was he admitting this to Roach? Precisely for that same reason, knowing that otherwise, the police would never have found the car and therefore, he could not be credited with so cleverly re-stealing it. But whatever the motive for carrying out the act, or for confessing it, this is how he did it.

Having followed the low-loader to see where the BMW was being kept, Martin realised that the biggest problem in retrieving it was the flat tyre. So he retired to a restaurant in Finchley Road, telephoned the AA, told them he had a slow puncture in one of his car's tyres and asked them to deliver a 'ReadySpare'. This was an appliance, manufactured in the US state of Illinois which distributed a TPMS (tyre pressure monitoring system) which really should have been used to inflate under-inflated spare tyres; however, for Martin's purpose, this would be more than adequate. The AA arrived with the appliance and Martin and Norman-Phillips waited near to the police station, which was manned twenty-four hours per day, seven days a week, until it was quiet. At about two o'clock in the morning, it was. Officers who had taken early refreshments at one o'clock had left to resume their patrols; the officers taking late refreshments had just gone into the police station. The two thieves crept in, inflated the tyre and since electronic ignition was in its infancy and the police had been advised not to tamper with it to try to immobilise it, Martin used the key which BMW Concessionaires had thoughtfully provided him with, and drove the car out of the yard.

In a nearby car park, they changed the registration plates for a further set of false plates, drove the car to Dover, thence on to a ferry bound for Calais and upon arrival at the French port, drove it on to Paris, where the car was dumped at Orly Airport. However, it was thought that this was not an isolated incident; it was believed that Martin had 'rescued' other cars which he had stolen and which the police had had the impudence to reclaim.

So in addition to that admission regarding the BMW, Martin also admitted obtaining goods by means of stolen cheques and credit cards but was careful only to admit to offences that he knew the police could prove. The following day, Martin and Green appeared at Hampstead Magistrates' Court and were remanded in custody for a week.

Now, it was paramount to retrieve the stolen car. Martin had said it was at the car park at Orly but the airport possessed 3,959 parking spaces. It could be re-stolen by somebody else or it could form part of an agreement for it to be shipped out to a buyer, eager for a limited edition of a brand new BMW. A request to trace the car was made through Interpol. The International Crime Police Organisation had been formed in 1923 to provide mutual assistance between signed-up member countries and was then based at St Cloud, a suburb of Paris. Its counterpart at Scotland Yard sent a request for the car to be traced but hours passed without a reply. The real Interpol bore no resemblance to the 1959 television series *Interpol Calling!* in which during each of its thirty-nine, grainy, thirty-minute episodes, grim-faced, granite-jawed detectives raced about to bring about the arrest of top-class swindlers or seedy looking foreign coves who specialised in white slavery or distributed filthy drugs. The London office of Interpol at New Scotland Yard was known both as 'The White Man's Grave' and 'Sleepy Hollow' and wherever possible, a posting there was sedulously avoided by working detectives. Thousands of enquiries passed through the office every year; each was docketed and filed. The detectives posted there did not carry out arrests and many were not fuelled with ambition. An example of the slothfulness which pervaded many Interpol offices was when I requested the details of the owner of a Milan-based car: it took four months for Italy to reply.

It was high time for 'The Old Pal's Act' to be invoked. The chief security officer for British European Airways (BEA), who was a former CID officer, was telephoned. In turn, he passed on all the information available to his opposite number at Orly and within forty minutes, the car was found and the French police informed. However, although the French police were willing to keep an eye on the car, they would not remove it. It was time for round two of 'The Old Pal's Act' to be put into operation.

The Detective Training School had been opened at Hendon in 1936, and as the years passed, detectives from all over the world attended the courses and some firm friendships were forged. One of Roach's colleagues who had attended the Advanced Detective Course had become friendly with a senior officer in the French *Compagnies Républicaines de Sécurité* (CRS) or security police. The CRS was split into different companies, one of which was the motorway police which patrolled urban areas. A phone call was made and by the time Roach and Police Constable Don Arrowsmith, a Class I driver, arrived at the car park, there was a CRS officer, complete with side-arm, automatic rifle, grenades and radio, sitting on the bonnet of the stolen BMW.

The car was immobilised and the following day the two officers returned it to Calais, so Roach got his wish of having a ride in such a prestigious vehicle when Arrowsmith opened up on the A26-A1 Autoroute and during the 186-mile journey managed to achieve the car's top speed of 135mph.

Several bottles of scotch had been acquired to repay the senior CRS officer for his assistance; however, he had gone on leave and therefore, upon their return to West Hampstead police station, the bottles were utilised to commemorate the car's return. Within a very short space of time though, the officers would have little to celebrate.

Roach was waiting at Hampstead Magistrates' Court to obtain a further remand in custody for Martin and Green. He was impatient, because although his squad had been carrying out a great deal of work in his absence, there was still an enormous amount of urgent enquiries to be dealt with and he wanted the case remanded and out of the way. Roach went to the cells where he saw Green, who, looking downcast, asked him, 'Have you got David, yet?'

Suddenly, Roach realised there was no sign of Martin. The gaoler was spoken to; he had not checked Martin in. Brixton prison was approached; they confirmed that Martin had been collected by the prison van service. Each prisoner had been locked in an individual cell in the van – so where was he?

The matter was soon resolved. At that time, it was the practice for remand prisoners to be collected from the various remand prisons and taken to Gerald Road police station in Victoria where the prisoners would be sorted out and placed on to the vans which were to deliver them to the various Magistrates' Courts. Inside the prison vans were cramped, individual cubicles and Martin had jammed something flexible into the lock of his cell door as it was being slammed shut at Brixton and thus the tongue did not fully drop into the housing. While the staff were in the office at Gerald Road sorting out which prisoners went where, Martin simply pushed open his cell door, opened a securely locked roof light, squeezed his narrow frame through the gap, climbed over the police station's gate, and vanished.

He broke into a flat at 13–16 Craven Hill Gardens, W2 on 25 October and stole a passport, correspondence, two Barclaycards, a cheque book, thirty-five pieces of jewellery, a camera, two coats and a shirt – and also a car to take them away in. Three days later, he stole a Citroën and between 1 and 8 November, he broke into a flat at 59 South Edward's Square, W2 and stole a quantity of photographic and electronic equipment. It was while he was on the run that we had our encounter at Forest Gate; no wonder Martin was keen to avoid my company!

Meanwhile, Roach intensified his enquiries which quite apart from recovering more stolen property, now included searching for Martin. His parents' address at Finsbury Park was raided; Martin was not there, but more property stolen by him was, as well as seals and dies for forging passports and Green Card insurance forms. Colin Black told me that Martin used 'Liquid Metal' (a tube consisting of gallium-containing alloys with very low melting points which are liquid at room temperature) to copy a passport's embossed stamp from which he would make a very authentic looking die.

During the search of the flat at Langtry Road, among the items of property seized was an A–Z directory and an officer was given the job of scrutinising every page to see if there were any tell-tale markings that might reveal where offences had been committed, as well as the location of where stolen property might be stashed. Inside one particular page was a sketch showing a stream, a reference to garages and the Great Cambridge Road, together with the letters 'VW'. It took the officer two more days before he was fairly certain that he knew that the place he was looking for was situated in Cheshunt, Hertfordshire.

The garages were identified and by lying on the ground and raising the bottoms of the shutters, the officers saw a Volkswagen van in it. One of the partners of the managing agents for the garages was a Justice of the Peace; upon hearing from the officers that they believed that stolen property was in the garage, he accompanied them there and opened the door. The registration number of the Volkswagen minivan, EMM 173J, revealed that it had been stolen between 14 and 17 January 1972; later enquiries revealed that David Martin had been the person responsible.

Inside the van was a whole mass of stolen property and after examining it back at the police station, papers led the officers to a car park at Heathrow where they recovered a Citroën containing a large amount of photographic equipment, passports and chequebooks. More camera equipment was seized from the old North London Air Terminal in Finchley Road. And at West London Air Terminal they found an escape kit – chequebooks, credit cards and passports in another Citroën.

A receipt found in the flat at Langtry Road related to a safety deposit box at Harrods; a search warrant was obtained which revealed that the box contained chequebooks, credit cards and stamps, made up to forge entries in Post Office Savings Bank Books. These stamps neatly dovetailed with the Post Office books found at Wood's address. The gang had gone to various Post Offices, opened accounts in nominal sums and provided false names. The stamps were made up by using letter stamps, bound around corks with wire. They were set in the name of the Post Office and when they were inked and stamped gave a good facsimile of a genuine entry stamp. Amounts were entered in the columns with false initials and fraudulent withdrawals were then made: simple but highly effective and very lucrative. And in a cottage in Hertfordshire, local constabulary officers, acting on a tip-off from Roach's squad, discovered stolen hi-fi equipment.

Janet Norman-Phillips was still on the loose and it was known that she was using stolen Barclaycards and cheques to live on. Roach and his team were aware of the Barclaycards she was using, so the chief security officer at Barclaycard was contacted – he had previously worked with Roach on the Fraud Squad – and every morning the investigators were telephoned with her latest string of offences. On a large blackboard, they could chart her movements which, from Derby, went directly south to Southampton and then back to London. With luck, they would be able to determine the next area where she would strike and effect her arrest. In the event, her apprehension was carried out following a violent and dramatic incident – which had nothing to do with Roach and his team – by young officers who were not even aware of the existence of Martin, Norman-Phillips or anybody else.

On 2 January 1973, plain-clothes officers from Hyde Park police station had been detailed to carry out an observation in Hyde Park's underground car park, due to a spate of thefts of and from vehicles parked there. Officers included 25-year-old Temporary Detective Constable (TDC) John Kelly and Police Constables Wally Hammond, 30, and Mick Edwards, aged 31. They saw a white BMW enter the car park, driven by a woman – this was Janet Norman-Phillips. The car had been stolen by her between 12 and 15 November 1972 but the officers were not aware of this. However, Norman-Phillips was equally unaware of the officers' presence and she got out of the car and tried to open the boots of three other unattended BMWs. The officers stopped her and she stated that she was looking for a friend's car, since she wanted to leave a note under the windscreen wiper; however, her actions were not consistent with someone wanting to leave a friend a message at the other end of a car. She agreed to accompany the officers to the police station but said she wanted to obtain evidence of her identity from her car. It was a trick, and a good one; as soon as she was inside her car, she slammed the door, locked it and started the engine.

TDC Kelly flung himself across the bonnet, PC Hammond managed to smash the driver's window but Norman-Phillips put the car into gear and drove straight at PC Edwards who managed to fling himself out of the way. The car roared off, with TDC Kelly hanging on to the wing mirror and windscreen wipers with Norman-Phillips swerving the car from side to side in an effort to dislodge him. The car tore into Park Lane and then Norman-

Phillips swung the car hard right at Brook Gate and smashed into a crash barrier; she was travelling so fast that the impact caused Kelly to be hurled into the air, hitting the road twenty-three feet away; his shoulders were fractured in three places. The girl had been knocked unconscious, having hit her head on the windscreen as the result of the crash; but after a short spell in hospital, she was arrested and questioned. Her admissions to the officers resulted in the recovery of even more stolen property and she too was charged with a variety of offences, including the attempted murder of a police officer.

Martin had since been arrested and by now the crime squad were wise to his antics; they had discovered one of his escape ploys. 'His trick was to chew some paper when waiting to be booked in,' Colin Black told me, 'then he would place the wet wad of paper into the lock keep as he was placed in the cell; this would stop the tongue of the lock engaging into the keep. We always double-checked the cell door with him in custody.' Black and his colleagues would then be posted to sit outside his cell twenty-four hours a day – 'Very boring!'

Now, once more, Martin was remanded in custody. It had been a lengthy, complex and an extraordinary inquiry and Roach and his team had every right to be pleased with themselves. They had recovered over 900 items of property worth by today's standards in the region of £320,000 – and their expertise, plus the courage of the Hyde Park officers, would later bring well-merited commendations from the trial judge and the commissioner.

Most importantly, they had smashed a gang of sophisticated criminals, who individually and severally had been involved with conspiracies to steal mail, to obtain money from Post Offices by means of forged instruments and to pervert the course of justice, quite apart from the car thefts and burglaries of which Martin was the undisputed leader.

Let Eddie Roach describe just one example of Martin's cool nerve:

> One example of the audacity of David Martin took place when he broke into a Bentley saloon in an underground car park, under flats in Hampstead. He, in his normal way, cleared all of the papers out of the glove compartment, together with a bunch of keys. On studying the papers, he discovered a receipt for a private aircraft refuelling. The receipt was on an American Express account from which he saw the card was due for renewal in a week's time. He rang the American Express company, identified himself as the customer and said that as his card was due to expire shortly and he had to travel to the States, could they please send him a new one immediately? The next morning, he hung around the flat, saw the postman go up to the door, waited until the postman had gone, then he opened the door with the keys he had stolen, took the American Express letter, left everything else, closed up and left.

Now he had been re-arrested Martin was remanded in custody at Brixton prison; however, the man who boasted 'No prison will hold me!' had a reputation to live up to and on Wednesday 30 May 1973 it was put to the test.

Prison Days

Brixton prison in South London was not high-security in the way in which Belmarsh prison is, which was opened in 1991; it was simply a remand prison for housing prisoners awaiting trial. Built in 1820, it was intended to house 175 prisoners; on 30 May 1973 there were approximately 770 prisoners incarcerated at Brixton. 'D' wing housed twenty prisoners thought to be security risks – Martin was one of them.

Between 1968 and 1972 annual armed robberies in the Greater London Area rose from just twelve to sixty-five. During the previous few weeks a gang of determined, armed bank robbers – they were known as the Wembley Mob – had been arrested and charged with a number of those robberies in which a total of £1,250,000 had been stolen. They had been remanded in custody at Brixton and they were rightly apprehensive regarding their ultimate fate. One of their number, one Derek Creighton Smalls – known as 'Bertie' – had appeared at Harrow Magistrates' Court on 3 April and the rest agreed to give evidence against them. The gang decided not to wait to discover how compelling Smalls's testimony might be; they already had a shrewd idea. Outside help was needed for them and it was not slow in materialising.

Early that morning, two rented Ford Escorts with their ignition keys and their tanks full of petrol were left parked in Clarence Crescent, almost within walking distance from the prison and strategically placed to offer escape to all points of the compass. Newspapers had been folded over the steering wheels as an aid to instant recognition for the would-be drivers. These were the change-over vehicles needed for the escape. At 10 o'clock the initial escape vehicle, a white Ford Transit Rent-a-Van, was left in Lyham Road, close to the rear gates of the prison; thirty minutes later a Lambeth District Dustcart with a hydraulic tipper trundled through the prison's rear gates as it did every Wednesday morning and commenced collecting the waiting refuse bags.

At 10.50 a warder opened a cupboard to be confronted by three prisoners, two of whom were members of the Wembley Mob, and one of the gang, Micky 'The Fish' Salmon, pointed a gun at the warder and his keys were demanded; in fact, the gun was made of soap, blackened with shoe polish, together with silver paper to add to its authenticity but it was sufficiently realistic for the warder to hand over his keys to David Martin. He was not a member of the gang but he had been included because he had previously memorised the warder's keys and knew exactly which key fitted which lock; and accuracy and speed were essential for the execution of the plan.

Several of the gang were released and they rushed out into the yard and headed for the dustcart. In doing so, they left the doors behind them unlocked and other prisoners, not associated with the Wembley gang, also took the opportunity to escape.

Seventeen prisoners were now in the compound. Philip Morris, one of the Wembley gang, dragged the driver out of the dustcart's cab, climbed in, and as he turned the truck around, other prisoners leapt aboard. With the prison alarms wailing, the warders rushed out and several of the prisoners grabbed the shovels and brooms from the truck and used them to attack the prison officers; Morris put his foot down and the truck roared towards the rear gates. The truck smashed straight through the wooden gates and the line of warders who had assembled outside in Lyham Road would certainly have been badly injured or killed had the truck emerged any further into the street – but it didn't. The hydraulic arms of the tipper were in the raised position and they jammed into the overhead frame of the gates.

Eleven of the prisoners stumbled out of the truck and into Lyham Road where they fought a running battle with the warders. Bruce Brown and four more of the Wembley Mob got into the waiting Rent-a-Van, started the engine and put it into gear but neglected to release the handbrake; it gave warders sufficient time to smash the windscreen with their truncheons. As the five men scrambled out of the van, Brown threatened a warder with a club and was cracked over the head with a truncheon. He slid to the roadway, suffering from a fractured skull and the rest of the robbers appeared to lose heart and they too were herded up.

Meanwhile, the four dog teams assigned to the prison were all off-duty but because they and their handlers were housed in married quarters adjacent to the prison, upon hearing the commotion they rushed into the prison grounds, where savage hand-to-hand fighting was taking place and the dog handlers accounted for four of the prisoners who surrendered.

Other prisoners, including Martin, stopped a passing Toyota at the junction with Lyham Road and Chale Road, pulled the driver out and got in. A warder leapt on to the bonnet but before he could smash the windscreen, the car shot forward and he was thrown into the roadway. The Toyota collided with another car, driven by another escaped prisoner. Martin was obviously not privy to the existence of the two getaway cars parked in nearby Clarence Crescent because he by-passed them completely. After a mile, the prisoners abandoned the hijacked car, but Martin and another prisoner hailed a taxi. However, as they drove away, they were followed by a police helicopter; a police car blocked their way in Bedford Road, Clapham and following a fierce fight they too were recaptured. Two other prisoners got clean away.

A number of prison officers had been injured – the number of casualties, one of whom sustained a broken wrist, varied between twelve and nine – and as Detective Superintendent Roy Ranson of Scotland Yard, tasked to head the inquiry into the breakout, told Ivor Mills of ITN, 'They did a marvellous job, here; we can't commend them sufficiently.' Martin might not have agreed with these effusive comments; he was thrown into solitary and, according to prison folklore, savagely beaten up.

Eddie Roach was furious that Martin had escaped, albeit temporarily; he called for statements from the police officers who had arrested him and discovered that Martin had been dressed in light slacks, a shirt and a suede leather jacket with fringes in the sleeves. Unconvicted prisoners were allowed to wear their own clothes but this was a privilege, not a right. As a known escaper, the prison governor had housed Martin in the secure wing, but although in theory the governor could have insisted that Martin should wear prison issue clothing with yellow patches on the trousers, this was seldom if ever done at Brixton. Nevertheless, Roach submitted a report to the Home Office which probably coincided with the inquiry carried out by Superintendent Ranson and ensured that from then on Martin was handcuffed to two officers when he was conveyed to and from court.

The time had come for a reckoning with Martin and it arrived a fortnight later; he and his co-conspirators appeared at the Old Bailey before His Honour Judge Edward Clarke QC (described by defence lawyers as being 'fearsome') on an indictment containing thirty counts. All of the co-defendants – with the exception of Martin – pleaded guilty. Janet Norman-Phillips was sentenced to a total of three years' imprisonment, Clive Green to two years' imprisonment, Bruce Wood to twelve months' imprisonment and Hugh Bestic to Borstal Training.

Martin did not plead not guilty – he looked up from the book he was reading and simply told the judge, 'I do not recognise this court' and that being so, there was little reason to appoint counsel for the defence. It was a ridiculous (and not to mention provocative) way to behave but His Lordship simply smiled thinly and said, 'Very well, Mr Martin, continue reading your book' and instructed the clerk of the court to enter pleas of not guilty. His trial lasted just three days and it took the jury no time at all to find Martin guilty of everything and on 14 June 1973 he was sentenced to eight years' imprisonment.

In October 1974, the Wembley Mob who, the previous month, had been sentenced to very long terms of imprisonment, appeared at the Old Bailey to be dealt with for the Brixton riot and breakout. Telling them, 'This was a mass enterprise prepared with great skill worthy of a better cause,' the Recorder of London, Sir Carl Aarvold OBE, TD sentenced Michael Salmon, Danny Allpress, Bruce Brown, James Jeffrey and Philip Morris to twelve months' imprisonment, to run consecutively to their serving sentences.

Also in the dock was 27-year-old David Martin. He received the same punishment. He was now serving a nine-year sentence.

From an early age, Martin had dressed in his mother's clothes. As he grew older, he also grew out of his mother's apparel, and so acquired female clothing of his own and at some stage, possibly before or perhaps during his time in the penal system, he became bisexual. In those times, for those in authority – police and prison officers – this also marked him out as wayward. Martin liked to refer to himself as 'Davina Martyn' although he was known to the other prisoners as 'Dave the Rave' because, as one of them said, 'he was a raving pouf'. As such, he was mainly ostracised by the other (primarily heterosexual) prisoners who possessed the usual prison prejudices; less so, by the homosexual inmates.

In the grim, austere surroundings of a high-security prison his appearance was quite extraordinary; his shirt could not really be described as such – it was more like a blouse. Martin wore moccasins and his painfully thin legs were encased in painfully thin jeans. At five feet ten, he appeared taller due to the sparseness of his physique and his large hooked nose was framed by his long, flowing blond hair. The overall effect, in ornithological terms, gave him the appearance of a cross between a rather benign vulture and a gorgeously plumed bird of paradise. He formed several sentimental attachments and delighted in stealing away a willing partner from an already formed and stable relationship but only on the understanding that he, Martin, would be in total control of the situation. However, Martin's long, undulating golden locks and mincing gait also attracted the attentions of very large, muscular and predatory homosexual prisoners. Heterosexual inmates who possessed similar herculean physiques sensibly avoided any kind of encounter with these prisoners and while Martin might have dictated who did what to whom with more amenable partners, this was not necessarily the case in these invasive situations.

In addition, Martin could not in any way be regarded as 'a hard case'; because of his physical frailty, prison opinion was that 'he couldn't have a fight to save his life'. But the views of the mainly hard-line would-be escapers began to change radically after Martin began to display his expertise when it came to locks. He fashioned lock picks out of any available commodity, metal or plastic. Magpie-like, he would collect nails and paperclips to utilise them for future use. He said he needed to see a key only once to be able to make a facsimile, and this was no idle boast – it was a gift granted to many 'keymen', including 'Johnny the Boche' aka Leonard Wilde, later sentenced to twenty-three years' imprisonment for his part in the 1975 Bank of America robbery.

All the time prior to, during and after his incarceration, Martin was learning: studying alarm systems and the workings of locks. He dissected locks to discover their workings and in a pin tumbler deadbolt lock, he saw how the five to eight key pins stopped in the middle of the radius of the cylinder above the key wald. Martin learnt the use of hook picks, diamond and snake picks, as well as a torque wrench to open those locks.

Wafer tumbler locks, of the type used in jewellery display cases, purported to have six pins. Martin discovered they had none. In more complicated and expensive locks, Martin discovered which way to turn the tumbler and some locks contained two sets of pins, with the second set being known as the master pins. They required two different keys to open them; they soon did not represent a problem for Martin.

He studied electronic circuit boards for security devices. He saw that single zone circuits contained independent exit and entry delays, but also that instant zones, tamper zones and personal attack zones could be added. There were circuits with timed bell cut-offs and resets and he discovered how pressure mats and inertia sensors were used. He learnt about the workings of alarm control keypads and also that some premises had alarms fitted to their fire doors. These doors could be opened to allow access but they had to be shut afterwards; if they remained open longer than thirty seconds, the alarm would sound. Martin discovered how to neutralise these and other door alarms.

He arrived at Parkhurst high-security prison on the Isle of White in 1974 with good credentials, having just been moved from Albany prison – similarly high-security – from the other side of the island following an escape attempt. Yellow stripes down the sides of his trousers announced that he was an 'E' Man – a potential escaper. It wasn't too long before the 'potential' was removed from his description. Martin offered to make a key which would open all the gates in the jail for a group of latent escapers and in addition a key to fit a double lock; and he was successful. Over a period of months, one by one, the other would-be escapers dropped out of the plan, leaving Martin and one other prisoner. They had also acquired items of warders' clothing, bit by bit, which were skilfully altered to fit them. On the morning of the escape, Martin and his companion, dressed in their prison officers' uniforms, unlocked, walked through, then locked one door after another. The prison security camera followed their movements but all that could be seen, to all intents and purposes, were two warders going about their duties. First, one gate with a double lock was opened and relocked, and now they were in the compound. They walked through to the second and massive double gates which were unlocked and then secured and now in front of them was the perimeter fence. Martin produced a pair of bolt cutters which had been smuggled into the prison and started cutting his way through the fence to freedom. Almost, but not quite. Sod's Law intervened when a prison dog handler from nearby Camp Hill prison was walking past. The dog took exception to Martin trying to emerge from the hole in the wire, his handler sent out a call for assistance on his radio and once more, Martin was thrown into solitary.

His key had not been discovered, however. It was slipped inside a thin, cylindrical tube which also contained a hacksaw blade; the tube, in turn was slipped up his rectum. That night, Martin extracted the tube, partially sawed through the hinges of his cell door and the following morning, eased the door open, released his companion and opened the punishment block gate. They were spotted by a warder and taken back to solitary confinement. During the time he actually spent in his own cell – and that was little enough – he was still up to mischief, drawing plans of the prison on pieces of paper and leaving them on his bunk, knowing that in his absence, they would be found by the staff. To Martin, winding up the staff was a pleasant way of passing the time, as was referring to the IRA prisoners as 'thick paddies'. Since the IRA was maintaining a mainland offensive with an appalling loss of life, Martin knew that he could well rely on the rest of the mainly staunchly monarchic inmates to protect him against retribution from those intrepid freedom fighters, but he also enjoyed antagonising other prisoners with stupid, spiteful comments. Perhaps he felt that his expertise in neutralising locks and escape attempts would elevate his status and act as a barrier from receiving a pasting, but on several occasions matters came very close to his convex nose becoming concave.

One evening, when one of the warders was carrying out his rounds, he noticed that there was an echo on his personal radio and realised that this was only apparent when he passed the door of Martin's cell. This was reported immediately. Martin was roused from his slumbers and his cell was searched. It was discovered that he had rigged up an aerial to his transistor radio which he had managed to re-tune to the frequency used by the warders. Was this a plan for the future or was it part of his own amusement, to casually pass on snippets of the conversations he had overheard between the warders, leaving them to scratch their heads in bewilderment as to the source of his accurate information? Possibly a bit of both, but whatever the reason, the aerial was dismantled and the radio probably accidentally dropped and just as unintentionally trodden upon.

Within months, he was transferred to Long Lartin prison in South Littleton, Worcester which had opened in 1971 and a year later added security meant that this prison held the most sophisticated security systems in the country. Cells doors were opened electronically from the central control room; Martin managed to short-circuit a control panel and open his and his companion's cell door without it registering in the control room. Over a period of weeks, Martin carefully sawed through the bars of his companion's cell before they crawled through the aperture. Even so, although they had escaped from the wing, with all of the other security measures in place, they never really stood a chance of escaping from the prison and once more, Martin was returned to solitary. To date, no one has ever escaped from the prison. Martin was fully aware that escape was impossible; it was his way of showing contempt for the penal system.

Next, shifted to Gartree prison in Market Harborough, Martin and a fellow prisoner escaped from their cells and broke into the workshop. There, they unsuccessfully tried to weld together a ladder in order to scale the perimeter fences. Making adroit devices to open the most sophisticated of locks or bypassing the most ingenious electronic security systems in the country posed no problems for Martin; constructing a simple ladder did. They were found next morning drinking tea when the workshop employees arrived for work. A rather more grandiose scheme was enacted five years later when a hijacked Bell 206L helicopter sprung two prisoners from the exercise yard, neither of whom were Martin or his fellow prisoner.

This is because by then Martin had been released. He had lost so much of his remission that of his nine-year sentence, he served eight years and three months, much of it in solitary confinement.

Out of Control

Martin was released from prison on 16 September 1981 into a Britain which was now experiencing unemployment of 3 million, the highest since the 1930s. Almost a decade had passed him by. The disappearance of Lord Lucan in 1974 would have been of little interest to him, as would the kidnap and murder of an heiress named Lesley Whittle a year later, although her abductor and murderer, Donald Neilson, would later figure decisively in Martin's life.

Prior to his release in 1981, Martin might well have expressed sympathy with the Brixton rioters for attacking the hated police; the same year, he definitely would have felt empathy for Marcus Serjeant who during the Trooping of the Colour discharged six shots from a starting pistol at Her Majesty the Queen. Prior to starting a five-year sentence, Serjeant told his accusers, 'I wanted to be famous.'

As Lord Byron had said following the success of his poem *Childe Harold's Pilgrimage*, 'I awoke one morning and found myself famous' and that would equally apply to Martin. So too could the comments of Byron's paramour Lady Caroline Lamb, who noted in her journal that her lover was 'mad, bad and dangerous to know'. However, Martin's fame – or notoriety – would have to be put on hold until he had carried out a rampage of months of criminality. Then his name and photograph would be plastered over the front page of every newspaper in the country and his fame would be assured.

And yet when one examines the facts, there was no need for it. Martin's expertise in the world of locks and security devices was second to none. He could have gone to the great locksmiths – Yale, Chubb, Lowe and Fletcher – and advised them of his ability and given his glib tongue they would certainly have employed him on an advisory basis to demonstrate to them the weakness in their appliances and how to manufacture their locks so that they might become impervious to lawbreakers. Armed with that degree of skilfulness, he could have named his own price. And the same applied to the security companies of the day: Securicor, Group 4, Brink's-Mat. His ingenuity could have rendered their defences impenetrable.

Because of his genius in the world of security, Martin would have been highly prized and respected, he would have basked in the adulation of his employers and he would have revelled in displaying how clumsy and ineffective their previous efforts had been and how clever he had been in pointing out and strengthening their deficiencies. In addition, for a poorly educated young man of 35 with eight previous convictions and who had just completed a nine-year prison sentence, he would have quickly and legitimately become very well off. But this was no ordinary talented person being discussed; this was David Martin. At a time when ATMs (Automated Teller Machines) were still in their infancy, Martin boasted that he could breach their security; and he probably could.

He was angry with society at large and in particular with those members of the penal system who he felt had treated him so shamefully over the past nine years and had led to a great deal of time in solitary confinement and being shifted from one high-security prison to another. Of course, his misfortunes were entirely the consequences of his own actions but Martin was unable to accept this. He had always loathed the police whom he regarded as the enemy. Now his hatred for them intensified; within a few short months of his newly found freedom, Martin would display his detestation for them in stunning style.

But now that he was free, Martin determined three matters: first, he would obtain a great deal of illicit money; second, he would never go back to prison; and third, he would never place himself in a situation which he could not control. First then was the acquisition of money. Ideally, this had to be in cash; it would cut out involving a receiver to fence the stolen goods and incidentally minimise the possibility of betrayal. Therefore the most lucrative and speedy way was by means of armed robbery, but this presented a problem. Robbery would be a first for Martin.

He had listened attentively to the armed robbers that he'd met in prison, those who were masters of their art: quick, ruthless and professional. But none of them would have volunteered to have 'gone across the pavement' with Martin; his idea of carrying out a successful robbery would have been going into a bank and shooting dead an elderly woman customer. In that way, 'everybody else would do exactly as they're told' while he helped himself to the money, which is how he described his intentions to a group of incarcerated and incredulous time-serving blaggers, many of whom had elderly mothers. Putting a shot in the ceiling to focus the bank staff and customers' attention was one thing, they felt, but blowing a grandmother in half with a sawn-off shotgun was quite another. They were even less interested when he suggested carrying out the robbery in drag. He might – or might not – have intended screeching, 'Look at me!' at the top of his lungs to shocked passers-by but that would have been the inevitable conclusion. And in addition, armed robbers were inevitably physically strong and as hard as nails, something Martin was not.

No. 'Dave the Pouf' might to some have been an amiable companion in prison and he was well respected for his skills as an escape artist, but going 'on the plot' with him was regarded as being unthinkable. Martin was a loose cannon and a lone one. So for the time being he concentrated on what he was good at: burglary at commercial premises by neutralising alarms, plus house burglaries, stealing cash and jewellery. He stole chequebooks and credit cards belonging to both men and women; most burglars would have sold these on to fraudsmen to use and dispose of, but not Martin. He carried out the fraudulent transactions himself and, according to the gender of the owners of these items, dressed accordingly.

In January 1982, he broke into Colour Film Services, a film processing laboratory at 22–25 Portman Close, Baker Street, W1, possibly through the roof. If he did, it is possible that he discovered a spare set of keys and made impressions of them. Albert Seaman, a driver, had been collecting films from the company late at night when he noticed a light on upstairs in the premises. He went up to switch off the light when he saw someone whom he initially thought to be a woman, since that person had long, fair hair, was wearing a woman's coat, tapered trousers, Cuban-heeled women's shoes and was carrying a handbag. As he got closer, he then realised that it was a man he had confronted, and gasped, 'Who the bloody hell are you?' to be told, 'It's all right, mate, I'm security' and Martin walked off, checking the door handles as he went. Seaman was a fortunate man; the next person to challenge Martin at those premises would not be so lucky.

Between 26 and 29 March, he burgled the offices of Eurotell Security Specialists in Davies Street, Mayfair, W1 and stole an enormous amount of property: an antique sword, two recorders, a television set, a voice stress analyser, twelve belt recording systems, two transmitters, a burglar alarm, three answering machines, fourteen belt microphones, a riot helmet, two sets of handcuffs and a quantity of surveillance and security equipment and body armour valued at £20,000. It is not known if Martin ever donned the body armour with the intention of it deflecting a bullet but whether he did nor not, it was fortunate that it was never put to the test, since it was used for demonstration purposes only and would not have afforded him any protection. The following week, he broke into John Weiss & Son Ltd, 17 Wigmore Street, W1 and stole surgical equipment. In both of these burglaries the loot was extremely bulky, so he must have used a vehicle and quite possibly, some assistance. If that was the case, however, the identity of his accomplice(s) was never discovered.

To further his aims to become a blagger, Martin now needed to acquire firearms and this matter was resolved during the weekend of 10–12 July 1982. The highly respected gunsmiths Thomas Bland & Sons at 22 New Row, Covent Garden, had the most sophisticated alarm systems – even the light switches were alarmed – but in his most daring coup to date the shop's security features did not present a problem to Martin.

Over that weekend, during the hours of darkness, the alarm sounded at the gunsmiths and the police from Bow Street were duly dispatched. They checked the outside of the premises and when they found nothing amiss, they called the keyholder. When he arrived, he unlocked the shop and he and the police searched the premises. Everything was as it should be, so the keyholder re-set the alarm, locked the premises and he left, together with the police who marked up the message 'faulty alarm'. A little while later, the alarm sounded again. Once more the police attended, could find nothing wrong with the exterior of the property, so they again called the keyholder. Once more the premises were unlocked, entered and checked to find nothing untoward. It was decided that the alarm must be faulty so this time it was not reset and it was decided to leave it turned off until the morning, when the alarm company would be contacted to come and fix whatever problem existed. The keyholder apologised for inconveniencing the officers again and they went their separate ways, with the police returning to Bow Street to once again mark up the message 'faulty alarm'.

This was the moment that Martin had been waiting for.

Several days prior to this incident, a man had been seen at the side entrance to the premises, apparently repairing a lock. It was thought that the man must be a locksmith and so he was: his name was David Martin. This door not only gave access to the gunsmiths, it also afforded entry to a multi-occupancy business premises. The mortise lock which Martin had removed was a very secure five-lever Chubb lock. Martin removed four of the levers, leaving just one in the middle which would activate the lock, and replaced it. Therefore, the key belonging to the owners of Bland's would certainly lock and unlock the door; and so would any old Chubb key which Martin had in his possession.

And therefore, on the night of the burglary, Martin simply walked up to the door and unlocked it. This activated the alarm; Martin relocked the door and melted away into the shadows. After the police and the keyholder had attended the premises on two occasions, with Martin again triggering the alarm on the second occasion, they had done Martin's job for him; the alarm was now disabled. The way was clear for Martin once more to use his key to unlock the unalarmed door and help himself to twenty-four handguns, 975 rounds of ammunition, four gun slings, two gun belts, thirty-three holsters and a pair of Powder scales, valued at £4,105. There was, of course, no sign of forced entry, either to the premises or the vaults where the firearms and ammunition were stored. In an almost uncanny way, it was as though nobody had entered the premises – it was just that a very large amount of highly dangerous weaponry had disappeared, which, in the words of Prospero from Shakespeare's *The Tempest*, had 'melted into air, into thin air'.

At the same time, Martin also broke into Susan Deacon Associates, a public relations consultant's office which was part of the business complex at New Row, and stole a sheepskin coat, two sheepskin jackets, a hanging wardrobe, two tea towels and a blip game, valued at £701 – it was pretty small beer for someone of Martin's calibre but then he was not one to waste an opportunity.

Surrounded with a small arsenal, David Martin had now acquired a toughness that nature had not endowed him with. He was all set to go to war.

Next, Martin stole a Ford Granada from a car park at London's Heathrow airport. A few days later, on 29 July, this Granada was used during the course of a £25,000 robbery on a Brink's-Mat security van outside Lloyds Bank at Bucklersbury House, 83 Cannon Street, in the City of London. It was a crime not executed with Martin's customary aplomb and coolness when circumventing alarms while breaking into premises. In fact, it appeared that he acted with exemplary stupidity.

What follows is an account of the robbery, both from the bare facts of the case, plus information from an unnamed source.

Martin was the front-seat passenger in the stolen car, driven by an accomplice. This was no carefully premeditated, skilfully thought-out plan, such as Martin's blagging contemporaries in prison would have devised. The two simply cruised around until they saw a security van; it happened to be part of the Brink's-Mat fleet but it could have been any security company's van. Both men were armed with handguns stolen from the gunsmiths and both wore motorcycle crash helmets; Martin was in drag. As the guard, Edward Ernest Burns, was transferring a metal container containing cash to the bank, the men strolled across and without a word being uttered, from a range of six inches Burns was shot in the leg, seriously wounding him. A shot fired at a second security guard fortunately missed. Snatching the money, another gun which had not been used to shoot Burns was dropped on the pavement and both men drove off. However, a group of men who had been drinking outside a nearby pub had seen what had happened and threw pint glasses at the Granada; Martin calmly told the driver to turn around. As the car drove towards the men, Martin opened his nearside window and fired at the group, fortunately missing them. The car was later found abandoned a quarter of a mile away in an underground car park in the Barbican. The first part of the incident – the actual robbery – fitted in quite neatly to Martin's prison dictum: shoot someone and the rest would do as they were told. And the second part – firing at the public-spirited pub customers – demonstrated how out of control he was becoming. It was his arrogant way of rebuking impertinent people who had dared to show criticism towards him.

Around this time Martin had rented two safe deposit boxes and into them went some of the stolen firearms and part proceeds of his crimes. It was also during this period, on 2 August, that Martin broke into office premises at 30 Old Bond Street and among other items stole identification cards, marked APS Security. In fact, during the burglary the company's managing director was working late and had challenged Martin, who calmly told him that he was a security advisor who had been employed by the former tenant of the office and that his name was 'Demain'. Asked how he had gained entry to the premises, Martin replied that he had climbed the fire escape to the top floor and had entered through an unlocked door; he then had the impertinence to admonish the director for poor security. Martin then left and later inserted photographs of himself in the cards describing the bearer as a security advisor named 'David Demain'.

At that time, the managing director did not report the matter to police but what did arise from this incident was that the fire door which Martin claimed to have been unlocked when he entered the building was, in fact, locked. Furthermore, it could only be locked from the inside; however, Martin's explanation could well have been a hoax. It is also possible that the front door could have yielded to Martin's lock-picking skills – either that or a duplicate key had been used.

Also at this time, two night-duty security guards in a prestigious office block were surprised to discover that a lift in the premises was in operation and was stopping at every floor. Since they were supposed to be the only two occupants in the building, they were understandably concerned and waited until the lift descended to the ground floor, whereupon Martin stepped out, produced his 'Demain' security card and coolly informed them that he had been engaged to check their competence. During the following discussion, Martin castigated them for failing to discharge their duties properly since he had been in the premises for some time and had checked all the offices without once seeing them. The chastened guards humbly saw Martin off the premises and since he had been so calm and convincing, there was, of course, no question of the police being informed; however, to cover themselves, a note was made in the security office's night-duty diary.

The occupants of the two buildings – the company director and the two security guards – would, with hindsight, congratulate themselves on not being more assertive in confronting Martin and relieved that they were merely censured with words; later intelligence would reveal that since the burglary at the gunsmiths and whatever he was doing, Martin was permanently armed.

When he was not busying himself breaking into premises and rebuking the occupants, Martin frequented gay bars and when he did so, one of the stolen pistols was inevitably in his handbag, with another tucked into his waistband. He was fiercely arrogant and keen to flaunt his sexuality at every possible opportunity. This was undoubtedly assisted by the growing strength of the gay movement during his enforced absence from society. In addition, gay clubs were rapidly opening up: Fangs, underneath a hotel in Paddington, was launched in 1975, as were one year later Bang in Charing Cross Road, Shane's in West Hampstead, The Catacombs in Earls Court and Heaven, situated under the arches beneath Charing Cross station. Boy George and Culture Club had appeared on BBC television's *Top of the Pops* and, for many, frequenting gay bars, cross-dressing and bisexuality was increasingly acceptable. In particular, Martin was a regular at The Embassy Club in Old Bond Street which had opened in April 1978. It was described thus:

> The door policy was strict but democratic; contemporary icons, freaks and beautiful people were invited in and those who did not fit into the scene were kept out. The mixed white, black, straight and gay crowd was a melange of glamorous drag queens, leather-clad gays and girls draped in gowns by Halston, Gucci and Fiorucci. Everyone took part in the disco tradition of dressing up to go dancing.

It was said that 'going to The Embassy was like being in a Hollywood movie with everyone wanting to be the star'; and that being the case, Martin must have felt as though he'd died and gone to heaven.

He was also involved in the making of pornographic films; he broke into film processing companies and stole their cameras and video recording equipment. And this was how, for the second time, he came to make an illicit entry into Colour Film Services, 22–25 Portman Close, Baker Street, shortly before midnight on 5 August 1982.

On the Run

On this occasion, Martin was seen in the first-floor office by Ken Trebeck, a night supervisor who was making a routine call to the premises, who not unnaturally wanted to know what he was doing there. Martin replied that he was 'security' and that he was there by arrangement with a director of the company. Although Trebeck appeared to accept his explanation, he went to another office where he quietly telephoned the police. When they arrived, Martin was calmly sitting at the reception desk using the telephone and told the police officers that he was a security officer named David Demain and showed them his identification. He produced a bunch of keys, unlocked the door to the office, went straight to the light switches and the officers followed him inside. The supervisor who had discovered Martin on the premises decided to telephone a director of the company; with incredible nerve, Martin asked to speak to the company's director, saying, 'There's an arrangement with another director; it's all hush-hush because we have had workmen in who left the fire escape open.'

However, one of the remaining officers went to his car to check out on the radio details of 'Demain' and the security company. Police Constables Nicholas Carr and Jerry Fretter stayed with Martin, questioning his story. In fact, 37-year-old PC Carr should not have been there at all; he was one of the late-turn shift who should have finished duty at 10 p.m. Instead, he had been at St Mary's Hospital reporting a personal injury accident; a woman had attempted suicide and when he completed his enquires, he had phoned Marylebone Lane asking for a lift back to the station. He was picked up by PC Fretter; en route the GP (General Purpose) car in which they were travelling was one of those which responded to the call.

The local area car also arrived; PC Fretter went into the premises with Police Constable Ian Hunter, the car's RT operator while PC Carr remained with the car's driver, Police Constable Dick Cross. An inspector and a female sergeant who were patrolling together arrived at the premises, accepted Martin's explanation and left, saying, 'there was nothing in it'.

But as Nick Carr told me, 'Ian Hunter came out of the premises, shaking his head. "There's something funny about him," he said.' Carr went into the building where with Fretter he saw Martin in the office. 'He was very calm, very well dressed and had keys to the premises,' said Carr. Martin once more said he was employed by the managing director and gave the officers the director's phone number; but when police called the number, the director's wife said he was out.

Martin now became agitated and the officers were unhappy with Martin's behaviour and told him to turn out his pockets; Martin refused, saying that he had done nothing wrong. 'He said, "You can't keep me here, I'm going,"' Carr told me, and the whole scenario was highly suspicious. 'I told him, "You'll spend three days in the cells and then we'll find out who you are,"' Carr recalled, and informed Martin he was under arrest, who promptly made a dash for it. The officers grabbed him and Martin pulled a pistol from his waistband. Carr, at six feet two and weighing thirteen stone, a tough former member of the 44th Parachute Brigade (V) recalled, 'I went to his right side and grabbed his wrist. The gun went off and I pointed the gun away from Fretter. There was a second shot and the third went into me.' The bullet had hit Carr in the top of his leg, near the groin. The officer crashed to the floor and Martin fled, shouting, 'Move, and you'll get another!' PC Carr, a qualified first-aid instructor, pressed down hard on the wound with both hands; it went a long way to saving his life.

Police Constable Perrie, who had been checking Martin's false particulars on the radio, heard the sound of three shots, left the car and ran towards the building where he saw Fretter, who exclaimed, 'He's got a gun – he's shot Nick!'

'Everyone turned up,' said Carr. 'The FME,[1] the TD[2] car and the DPG[3] arrived,' and so did Detective Constable Fred Arnold who was the night-duty CID officer covering the whole of 'D' Division. 'I ran up the stairs,' he recalled, 'and saw PC Carr being gently positioned for removal by the paramedics to hospital. One of the paramedics was firmly holding PC Carr's finger in the wound as PC Carr's condition was weakening. This plugging of the wound prevented a more serious outcome as PC Carr looked very grey and poorly.'

Carr was taken to the Middlesex Hospital where it was discovered that the bullet had severed the femoral artery, responsible for the main arterial supply to the lower limb. The artery was tied off and after an hour-long operation, the skilful surgeons stabilised his condition; however, PC Carr had lost six pints of blood. 'The bullet had bounced off the hip bone, went down the line of the groin and ended up between the hip bone and the knee,' recalled Carr. He was hospitalised for several weeks.

The offices at Colour Film Services were sealed and became a crime scene; an incident room at Marylebone police station

---

1. Force Medical Examiner.
2. Traffic Patrol.
3. Diplomatic Protection Group, who were always armed.

was set up the following day and an investigation commenced under the direction of Detective Superintendent George Ness, the deputy head of 'D' Division's CID. Detective Sergeant Tom Martin was the office manager and the staff included Detective Constables Fred Arnold, Stuart Smith and Peter Finch as well as some temporary detective constables and two female officers.

'He may have been a video pirate,' suggested Ness in a press interview, 'as the firm is concerned with video and is in the process of setting up a new venture which is to copy video tapes on a large scale.' However, he also emphasised that the intruder was highly dangerous, adding 'A man who carries a gun and is prepared to use it can only be called a potential killer.'

The hunt was on for 'David Demain', but who was he? Nobody seemed to know. No one by that name was listed on the local electoral roll, nor in the telephone book. A search for that name in the 'Nominal Index' at the Yard's Criminal Record Office (CRO) was conducted, without success, as was a search at CRO's 'Method Index' for any likely suspects who fitted that description. If, when Martin had been previously arrested, he had used the alias of Demain, this would have been listed at CRO under the 'Miscellaneous Nicknames and Aliases Index', but he hadn't, so it wasn't.

A description of the gunman was circulated on an 'All Stations' message and the collators' indices of the surrounding stations were unsuccessfully searched for a 'David Demain'. Although Martin had been born in Paddington, he had been out of circulation from that area for many years. In fact, many of the officers had not served at Paddington Green when Martin was active in that area; some had not even joined the police. Police informants were urged to provide information as to the gunman's identity but this was met with a conspicuous lack of success; Martin was a loner.

The police could not raid houses in their hunt for Demain, because they did not know whose houses to search. Neither could they apply for the necessary permission to intercept telephone calls or postal mail, because they were unaware of whose telephone calls or letters to monitor. They were stymied for the lack of a name and an address. In fact, Martin had fled to his luxuriously appointed rented penthouse flat, no more than half a mile from the scene of the crime.

Naturally, following the shooting, the occupier of the premises at Old Bond Street who had confronted Martin a few days previously was interviewed by police; he provided the investigators with the details of the previous tenant, Peter Sarony, a registered gun dealer with premises at 44 Harrowby Street, W1 and he too was questioned, but he knew nobody by the name of Demain.

Ten days later, though, there *was* someone who knew that name: the foreman at Pickfords' warehouse at Fulham who received a telephone call from a Mr Demain who wished to store some items in that depositary. The following day, 16 August 1982, these items were delivered and there were a lot of them: four laundry baskets, five tea-chests, a two-drawer filing cabinet and a large cardboard box, all of them full. Although the foreman was unaware of it, these receptacles contained a large amount of property stolen by Martin during the course of three of the burglaries, including shoulder holsters, security and surveillance equipment and medical items.

Of course, the police were not aware of this, and were unacquainted with the person who had deposited them. Her name was Susan Stephens, a 25-year-old former model and dancer who lived at 29 Victoria Road, Kilburn. She was also Martin's girlfriend but this intelligence had not been passed to the police, since they were also unaware of Martin's identity; in any event, Miss Stephens had identified herself to the staff at Pickfords as Miss Freeson, a name she had used as a model. Stephens had first met Martin, probably in May 1982, possibly at

The Embassy Club and had occasionally gone out with him. He seemed, she would later say, 'besotted' with her and in November, she would move into a flat at West End Lane, Hampstead. The incriminating evidence remained undisturbed at Pickfords for the next five months. Meanwhile, since Martin had unaccountably and fortuitously come into a great deal of money, he and Miss Stephens were off on a month-long holiday in Ibiza.

Almost six weeks had passed since PC Carr had been shot and the lukewarm trail had grown cold. Then, on the morning of 15 September 1982, a customer entered Armalon Ltd, the gun dealer's premises at Harrowby Street whose owner had previously been interviewed by the police, and purchased some special 'Pachmayer' pistol grips. He also wished to purchase a 9mm magazine but since this was not immediately available, he placed an order for it. Mr Sarony politely requested contact details from the buyer and just as courteously, the customer provided a telephone number and his name, and left the shop. The name he had given, 'Demain', instantly rang alarm bells with the dealer who promptly passed the purchaser's details and his description to Detective Constable Peter Finch at Marylebone Lane police station.

Now the police had a very promising lead. A check on the telephone number revealed that it was an 'Aircall' number; it related to an answering machine situated in an inspection pit, at the bottom of a lift shaft in Wigmore Street, W1. From the 'Aircall' company they obtained an address: flat no. 16 on the seventh floor of 1–3 Crawford Place, W1.

Initially, just two officers, Police Constables Steve Fletcher and Steve Lucas, were sent to the flats; neither armed. Fletcher told me:

Steve and I found the front door on the first floor at the back. We sat for a few hours, not very well concealed, nattering and smoking fags. We were later relieved by a team of four officers; I think two of them were armed. One of the armed officers was PC Peter Van-Dee, another crime squad colleague. Peter was an interesting man. He had dual nationality – United States and British. I think he had served in the Met, left and joined the police in America – Portland, Oregon, from memory – he then returned to the UK and rejoined the Met.

More officers, some of them armed, from the investigating team quickly surrounded the flat. Others were on the roof and more in the surrounding streets.

At about 9.40 that evening, Martin, who had arrived back in the United Kingdom three days earlier, turned up at the block of flats; but the officers were unaware of it. Police Constable Steven Lucas (who had earlier been relieved from duty but had now returned) and Detective Constable Peter Finch were on the seventh floor when they saw what they assumed to be a woman, carrying a black handbag walking along a long corridor. As PC Lucas would later tell an Old Bailey jury:

> This person had long fair hair and a striped yellow T-shirt and was wearing trousers. The person looked effeminate. At first, we stood back, believing it to be a woman but then we approached and DC Finch said, 'Excuse me, love …' The person was standing by the door, about to put a key in. She turned round and it was David Martin. He was holding a large black handgun and at that point, DC Finch grabbed him bodily.

As the officer struggled with Martin, he shouted, 'I'll have you – I'll blow you away!' DC Finch shouted to the other officers who were on the roof and they were quickly joined by Detective

Sergeant Tom Martin, Detective Constables Jim Francis and Fred Arnold and also Police Constable Peter Van-Dee.

Martin, who was struggling furiously, suddenly dropped the black Smith & Wesson .38 Chief Special revolver (which was loaded with five bullets and had been fitted with the Pachmayer grips, purchased earlier that day) and appeared to surrender. Instinctively, Finch relaxed his grip; it was the moment Martin was waiting for. He produced a second firearm, a silver Star 9mm self-loading pistol, loaded with fifteen rounds, with one in the chamber, ready to be fired, from his waistband and pointed it at the detective. PC Lucas shouted, 'He's got a gun!' and PC Van-Dee, having no doubt that he was about to witness a colleague being murdered, shouted 'Freeze, armed police!'

'Pete [Van-Dee] later told me that, convinced Martin was going to shoot, he drew his service revolver, placed the barrel against Martin's head, looked aside and pulled the trigger,' Steve Fletcher told me. 'He told me, everything froze for a split second. He looked back, expecting to see "strawberry jam" (Pete's words) where Martin's head had been. Not so. He resumed his struggle, slightly less ferociously than before as his collar bone was broken. It transpired that the bullet that Pete fired pierced Martin's scalp, then travelled down between skin and bone, down to his shoulder, fracturing the collar bone.'

Both Martin and Finch crashed to the floor, with Finch on top, but still Martin continued to kick out and at the same time, with his right hand, tried to grab one of the two handguns. Finch, by now almost exhausted, drew his gun and hit Martin in the face with it. DS Martin, who had also drawn his revolver, ran up and swept the two handguns away. Apparently, Finch was initially annoyed at Van-Dee for firing his revolver, thinking that he too could have been shot, but in the circumstances there was little else that the officer could have done. As Finch told me, 'Peter

[Van-Dee] told me afterwards that the end of the barrel was close to my head and that's why he fired his gun.'

In spite of being shot, Martin continued to fight ferociously, even after being handcuffed, telling the officers, 'I could have killed the lot of you, I could have had you all! Why don't you just finish me off?' And then, as Fred Arnold recalled, he looked the officers in the eyes and said, very calmly, 'You cunts can't do anything right. Come on, give me another one.'

Other officers who had been in nearby Macready House, a police section house, rushed to the incident, including the then Police Constable 532 'D' Martin Power, attached to the crime squad. As a crew member of 'Q' Car, 'Delta One-one', he had been one of the first on the scene when PC Carr had been shot. The sight that confronted him now was that of David Martin, with blood pouring from him, with officers trying to restrain him. 'My DS appeared and told me to get a first-aid kit,' recalled Power. 'I ran down as the area car, 'Delta-one' turned up and grabbed the kit; when I got the kit up to Martin, the DS tied his legs together with a bandage!' Martin's legs needed restraining; he had kicked DC Arnold in the face and chest, causing him to fall awkwardly, resulting in injuries to his back, rear ribs, spine and shoulder which later required surgery.

A resident on the same floor offered Finch a large scotch; 'Greatly appreciated!' he told me and a couple emerged from a nearby flat and offered the use of their telephone; an ambulance was called and DC Jim Francis telephoned Inspector John Devine, Marylebone's duty officer, who arrived and saw Peter Finch. 'I could see he was covered in blood spatters and not really "with it",' recalled Devine and arranged for Finch to be taken back to the police station. Finch had acted commendably. In justifiably hitting Martin in the face with his revolver, he made no secret of it and included this incident in his notes and later his statement. However, during the next twelve months, and through no fault of his own, things were to go badly wrong for Finch and this incident would be the subject of profound criticism at Martin's trial.

Detective Sergeant Roger Clements had been part of the inquiry ever since PC Carr had been shot. He had been night-duty CID at the time, but following that tour of duty, he recommenced running the Crime Squad at Marylebone Lane police station and took some of his forty-two young charges to hunt for PC Carr's attacker. Now, he accompanied Martin to St Mary's Hospital, Paddington.

By now, Martin was raving. 'I could have shot them all,' he exclaimed. 'I made a mess of it. I could have had four or five of them!' However, raving or not, because of the amount of blood covering Martin, Clements began administering a 'Dying Declaration', a statement only to be taken when a person is in imminent danger of dying, beginning with the ominous words:

> I, (name) having the fear of death before me and being without hope
> of recovery make the following statement …

But then Clements looked up to see a doctor, standing behind Martin, shaking his head. 'He's not going to die,' said the doctor. Clements took possession of Martin's clothing; underneath the trousers and the T-shirt, he was wearing stockings and women's underwear. When questioned about it, he replied, 'It's my scene.'

If Martin was not by now actually kicking, he was certainly alive and before he went into surgery, he demanded to know,

'Why didn't you finish me of? Looking at it logically, with four armed coppers in those circumstances, I should be dead. Unfortunately, you didn't do your job properly and I am not dead – you fucked up!' But PC Van-Dee had not 'fucked up' at all. He had reacted precisely as he had been trained. Let's pause to consider gun statistics at that time.

During 1981, police had been issued with firearms on 4,983 occasions and had drawn their revolvers 106 times, firing just six times during two incidents where no one had been hit. Criminals, on the other hand, had used firearms on 1,168 occasions. But gun crime was worsening; now in 1982 criminals had used firearms 2,069 times and police had been issued with firearms on 6,635 occasions and drawn them from their holsters 118 times; during that period, police had opened fire six times, injuring three people. Martin was one of those casualties and, given the circumstances, no one was going to blame PC Van-Dee for his actions. Indeed, his feat had been praiseworthy in the same way that Finch's achievement had been commendable. In addition, Martin had also been in possession of a clip containing a further fifteen rounds for the Star pistol, plus ten more rounds for the revolver. Martin's response was nothing more than an extension of his enormous ego. Before he had admonished security guards for failing to discharge their duties; now he was castigating Peter Van-Dee for neglecting to kill him. With Martin, he was always right; it was everybody else who was in the wrong.

According to a later newspaper interview, Sue Stephens had arrived outside Martin's flat, only to see a police officer outside. 'I knew something was wrong,' she accurately stated. 'I just legged it.' Even though Martin had been shot from the closest possible range and had lost a considerable amount of blood, he made no mention of pain or indeed any discomfort. The consultant surgeon was astonished that Martin was not suffering from any form of trauma, and concluded that Martin had not been seriously injured and the doctors agreed that he was fit to be interviewed by police. Shortly after Martin's admission to hospital, he was interviewed by Detective Superintendent Ness and Detective Inspector Bob Cook. Martin declined to have legal representation present while he was questioned and refused to answer any questions at all. Bob Cook told me, 'His egotistical, boastful character was quickly evident. After the interview, he bragged about his ability to escape from custody, police or prison, claiming that no one could hold him once he had made up his mind to escape.'

Answering questions or not, Martin, in hospital under armed guard, continued his boastful ravings to anyone who would listen. 'I got to the door and heard a noise. I looked around. Your bloke was there. I should have taken him out there and then. I could have got away easily. I could have taken out four or five and all the rest would not have wanted to know.' In fact, once again, Martin was using the dictum he had previously expounded, about shooting a customer in a bank 'and then the rest would listen'; it had been utilised in the shooting of the security guard in the City of London robbery, plus firing a shot at another guard. Telling his listeners that he had two guns with him, one in his handbag, another in his waistband, he was asked if he would have used them and he replied, 'Yes. I don't know why I didn't. I wouldn't be here now, if I had. I went for my gun and he dived on me and the others followed. It's all a bit hazy. We struggled.' He said that while he was going for his second gun, there was a bang. 'I knew I'd been hit. It's a funny feeling, really.'

However, the investigation as to what he had been up to had got underway and Martin would find that the result of those enquiries was anything but funny.

Escape Plans

'David Demain' had now officially been identified as Martin and an in-depth search of his flat at Crawford Place got underway. The wardrobe, full of women's dresses, leather trousers, sling-back shoes and designer underwear, caused raised eyebrows among the detectives but there were far more interesting matters to excite their attention. A leaflet was found relating to a safe deposit box service; keys in Martin's possession fitted the locks of the boxes which he had rented two months previously. In both were a veritable treasure trove of valuables and evidence. The first, rented from Selfridges, Oxford Street, W1 contained £3,595 in cash, foreign currency and jewellery as well as seven of the handguns together with ammunition that had been stolen from Thomas Bland & Sons. The second security box, which had been rented from the Berkeley Safe Deposit, Davies Street, W1 contained £2,000 cash, three APS identity cards – all bearing Martin's photograph – plus four more handguns and ammunition. A signatory to the box was one 'Danja Thyssen', coincidentally a name used as a model and dancer by Susie Stephens.

A car key was found in Martin's possession; it was traced to a Mercedes which had been stolen from the car park at Heathrow on 24 July, at the same time that the Ford Granada had been taken. There were also documents relating to a Volkswagen Golf; this, together with an Audi, had been stolen between 19 and 30

April from Vag (UK) Ltd, Manston Road, Ramsgate. The Audi was later recovered while in possession of two men, associates of Martin, who were charged with the theft of the vehicle and were bailed to attend Ramsgate Magistrates' Court; they failed to appear. The Volkswagen was later found in Calais. It was searched by the Sûreté Nationale and five more handguns, stolen from the Covent Garden gunsmiths, were found; forensic tests identified that one of them had been used to shoot the security guard in the £25,000 robbery in July. Another identified the gun, a .22 revolver, which had been used to shoot PC Carr.

On 22 September, Martin was discharged from hospital. He was taken to Paddington Green police station where a series of identification parades were held. 'This had to be the straightest ID, ever,' Carr told me. 'Officers from other stations ran the identification parade and there was someone on the parade who was an absolute dead ringer for Martin.' It did not deter Carr plus several other officers from correctly identifying Martin; in fact, at Martin's later trial, identification did not become an issue for the defence.

Detective Constable Jim Francis was part of the investigating team and during a boastful moment, Martin chillingly told him, 'I've just done nine years for fraud. You don't get that much for murder – and you're next!' Although Martin was not amenable to official questioning, it was thought that he might be induced to impart information with a series of informal 'cell chats'. It was Detective Constable Fred Arnold deputed for this duty; notwithstanding being kicked in the face by Martin, it was thought with justification that Arnold would be the right man for the job. The six foot five former Royal Marine Commando had enjoyed a considerable number of successes during his career. Arresting an ex-mercenary for the murder of a neighbour, the man was induced to admit another thirty-nine crimes committed throughout the country. And after a two-week nationwide hunt for the man who had shot and paralysed Police Constable Philip Olds QGM, the time taken for Arnold to receive a tip-off, arrest and deposit the gunman at the police station was just thirty minutes, the same amount of time it took for Martin to write the gunman's full confession and book off duty by 10 p.m.

'He did not come across as thuggish, heavy or behave in a cocky manner,' Arnold told me:

> He was not into physical stuff but would shoot people with pleasure. He was cool, calm and calculating. He rarely swore, did not smoke or drink and was always calm in the presence of police. He was mean and extremely clever. He was a career criminal; he worked alone but could always call on a selection of other criminals for specific crimes. These criminals were in awe of him and feared him. I spent more conversation time with him than any other officer and I found him interesting and most certainly different. He insisted throughout that he was not a criminal but a businessman and his wages/earnings came from shooting Securicor guards as they entered bank premises with containers of money. Simple. He was deadly serious and could not understand why the police thought this was criminal.

Arnold was told to 'try to get into him' in order to recover the unaccounted for firearms from the gunsmiths burglary, in the event that they were now in the hands of other underworld figures, and in addition, to determine whether or not he was accompanied during the burglary. However, Martin would not explain how he had broken into the gunsmiths, and he would not admit to any other person being involved. Time after time, Arnold brought this matter up, hoping that Martin would deviate from 'I' to 'we' but he never did. And when he was asked why he had taken so many guns, his stock answer was, 'That was all I could carry.'

Arnold was also tasked to take a statement from Susie Stephens, which, over a period of several hours, he did. Her identity had been established after she visited him at the police station and she would continue to visit him at Brixton prison and at court. He told me:

> In her statement, she mentioned an overland trip/holiday they took in a stolen VW car with false plates to Ibiza. They used a system of ferries to reach Ibiza. In Ibiza, they stayed in a hotel; Martin only ever used cash. They photographed each other posing with handguns ... The flat where he was staying was searched and amongst the items of interest that were found were a number of film processing receipts to be collected from a Boots Chemists in Knightsbridge. I collected the processed films and some of the photos clearly showed both of them posing with handguns. The stolen car was abandoned on returning from Ibiza in a car park in Calais near to the ferry terminal. Martin felt it was too risky to enter Dover in the stolen VW in which, of course, the stolen handguns from the burglary were found.

Arnold also supervised visits between Martin and Stephens at the police station. 'They were allowed no contact and I sat between them on all visits. Other officers covered the cell passage area,' remembered Arnold. 'The visits were rather subdued and on one visit, Martin became very emotional and tears welled up in his eyes and he lowered his head in silence; I don't know why. But he really did have some feelings towards Sue Stephens. Maybe he felt she was the only person in the world he could trust.'

This was possibly one of the few times in which Martin did display compassion. During one of the informal 'cell-chats', Arnold posed a hypothetical question to him, asking what would his reaction be if, when driving a stolen car, he were to be stopped and questioned by a woman police officer? Martin's reply was calm and unequivocal: 'I would shoot her dead, if need be.'

Martin was charged with attempting to murder PC Carr, plus fourteen other firearms, robbery and burglary charges. He appeared at Marlborough Street Magistrates' Court and was remanded in custody.

Robert Darby was a uniformed police constable at Marylebone and, as he admitted to me, 'I always felt uneasy in his presence. He was a very cold person who refused to make eye contact with you.' Before leaving for court, Darby supervised Martin washing himself. 'He was meticulous about cleanliness,' he told me, 'particularly with regard to his nails which were quite long.' Martin's nails would figure in a strange episode that followed. There were a few officers who treated Martin in a relaxed manner, but not Darby; he had not forgotten what had happened to Nick Carr, especially since he had been the best man at Carr's wedding as well as collecting and rushing Carr's wife to the hospital on the night of the shooting.

Fred Arnold organised Martin's conveyance between Brixton and court and his return. He and two temporary detective constables would drive to Lambeth police garage, meet the driver of the seven- to eight-seater prison van with clear glass windows and thence to Brixton prison. The van was always accompanied by Arnold driving his authorised vehicle, a Honda Accord, either in front or behind. Martin incessantly looked out of the windows at the roads they were travelling along, the buildings, the side streets. As they drove north along Brixton Road, they turned left and crossed the junction with Clapham Road, on towards Vauxhall, then north again along the Albert Embankment. All the time, Martin's eyes were flickering from side to side, up and down, perhaps weighing up chances, evaluating the route; then across Westminster Bridge, up Whitehall, on to Piccadilly Circus and up Regent Street until, just before Oxford Circus, turning right into Great Marlborough Street.

Martin always had a magazine to read in the van but on one occasion, Darby suddenly noticed that Martin was scratching at the magazine with his long nails and he snatched it away from him. He saw that what Martin had been scratching was the registration number of Arnold's car. Darby immediately brought this to Arnold's attention who replied, 'By the time he gets out, I'll have bought another car.' Arnold later told me, 'I wasn't alarmed by the occurrence but observed him intently, at all times. I felt it best to monitor all that Martin did to get further into his character as he was so clever and devious.'

There were other indentations made by Martin's fingernails which were indecipherable. It was thought that these might have been some sort of code in connection with an escape attempt. Information was received – and how reliable it was, was anybody's guess – that criminal associates of Martins were planning to attack the escort with Belgian pump-action shotguns to secure his release.

There are alternative explanations to the fingernail scratching on the magazine. First, that by acquiring Arnold's registration number, this could also lead to him accessing Arnold's home address, simple enough for someone of Martin's ingenuity. From there, this could lead to associates of Martin's kidnapping and threatening Arnold's wife and daughters in exchange for Martin's freedom and this is not as fanciful as it might sound; within three years, I would be dealing with a kidnapping where a family was kept tied up in their home overnight until the criminals' plans were satisfactorily carried out.

The second interpretation is that incorporating the information regarding the attack on the prison convoy was all a blind, a distraction, that this was disinformation, promulgated by Martin or at his instigation. In this way, everybody's attention would be focused on the journeys from prison to court. Once he was back at Brixton he would be treated as a security risk and since he had escaped from there ten years previously (plus other attempts at escape from other high-security prisons), no one was going to take any chances. And while he was at court, there would be sufficient police officers to ensure his detention in the dock and when he was in the cells he would be incarcerated there for the shortest amount of time. As he was to be remanded on each occasion, he would be dealt with first, returned to the cells and there would be no question of him waiting for the ordinary prison van to turn up; he had his own bespoke prison van waiting to whisk him back to Brixton.

So the route was varied and no such attempt to 'spring' Martin was made – but the fingernail indentations were an ominous sign which might mean something or nothing. Darby's assessment of the prisoner was that 'Martin was one man you couldn't give an inch to,' he told me. 'There was something scary about him.'

Three months passed. This was a long time between arrest and committal to the Old Bailey, where it was intended that Martin would stand his trial, but the police were meticulously assembling their case to ensure it was absolutely watertight. In addition, Martin was utilising delaying tactics. This was a common ploy, used by many manipulative criminals who knew there was no chance of bail. The reasons were multi-faceted; first, the amount of time that they spent on remand would be deducted from whatever sentence they ultimately received. Next, it afforded them days out of the remand prison. Also, they could extract enormous satisfaction from manipulating the system by making irritating and nonsensical demands. It was puerile behaviour but then it suited Martin, who possessed a shallow personality.

There was another reason. After being deposited at Great Marlborough Street court, Martin had become thoroughly acquainted with his cell. Initially, while waiting to go into court

Martin had been handcuffed to two officers in his cell. But as time passed and Martin appeared quiet and subdued at his court appearances, security grew lax and he went and stayed in his cell unaccompanied. Matters were going just the way he had planned them and Martin had plenty of time, therefore, to make his preparations.

It was the practice of the officers escorting Martin to arrive at court early, lodge him in the cell – always the same cell – and then go off for breakfast. And why shouldn't they? When the prison van entered the secure area behind the court building, the huge yard gates would be swung shut behind it and locked. Martin would then be taken in handcuffs down the metal staircase to the cells, the handcuffs would be removed, he would be placed in his own private cell, the door locked and bolted. From the metal staircase, one could clearly observe the structure of metal spikes around the roof guttering. It was difficult to imagine more robust security measures – and of course, Martin was safely ensconced in his cell.

He arrived at court on Christmas Eve 1982, and meekly allowed himself to be inserted into his usual cell for the twenty-eighth – and final – occasion. At 10.30 a.m. the jailers went to his cell in order to take him into court and were astonished to discover it was empty. As the escorting officers returned from breakfast, two of the court staff were on the pavement outside the court and one shouted, 'Martin's escaped from his cell!'

Martin had got out of his cell, into the corridor, gone to the top of the court, forced a skylight and made his way over the spikes and across the rooftops; all this, and remember, Martin had suffered a bullet wound which had smashed his collarbone just three months previously. He got in through a service door of the London Palladium theatre and walked downstairs. Martin looked at the theatre's empty 2,286 seats – by that afternoon, every one of them would be filled by a pre-Christmas audience to be entranced by the matinee performance of Michael Crawford playing the eponymous role in the musical *Barnum* – but nobody noticed the slim, fair-haired man as he padded down the stairs. At that moment, the only person topping the bill of the prestigious Palladium was that well-known escape artist David Ralph Martin.

Martin strolled out through the Palladium's foyer into Argyle Street, mingled very briefly with the last-minute Christmas shoppers – and vanished.

The Hunt

The balloon went up – as they tend to do on these occasions – and the investigating team from Marylebone had their Christmas leave cancelled and the manhunt for Martin got underway, this time from an incident room at Paddington Green police station. Simultaneously, an internal investigation commenced in which the unhappy gaoler at Marlborough Street court featured to determine precisely how Martin had escaped.

The Chubb Lock & Safe Company had since its inception in 1804 been justly proud of their appliances and since they supplied the locks for the cells at Great Marlborough Street court they sent a top team from their headquarters at The Chubb Building, Fryer Street, Wolverhampton to carry out a thorough examination of Martin's cell door. The lock was not damaged in any way and was in perfect working order. To them, Martin's disappearance was a complete mystery.

In November 1982, Susie Stephens had moved into a second-floor flat above a drinking club named 'Lately' at 175 West End Lane, Hampstead. Police were aware of this change of address because since Martin's £100,000 flat at Crawford Place had been recovered by the owners, Taylor Woodrow Ltd, Martin had authorised Detective Sergeant Tom Martin to restore some of the property, plus his clothing in the flat, to Stephens.

Within a very short space of time from Martin escaping, armed officers were at Stephens's flat searching for him, including Police

Constable John Barnie and an inspector. 'We searched the flat thoroughly,' he told me, 'including looking behind the bath panel and under the kitchen sink.' There was no trace of him but officers from the inquiry remained in and around the premises, working on the assumption that Martin would turn up. He didn't; but the boyfriend of Tracye Nichols, one of the other occupants of the flats, arrived for Christmas dinner and was mightily alarmed to have a detective leap out and point a gun at his head. He was not the only person to have their yuletide festivities disturbed; later that day Stephens went to visit her parents at the family home in Devon to discover that they too had received an unannounced visit from armed police officers and were understandably furious.

The likeliest places where Martin might go were raided, without success; this included his parents' address at Clissold Park. 'It was not the type of area where cats and dogs would willingly walk through,' wryly said former Detective Sergeant Roger Baldry, 'let alone human beings!' Baldry, who was then attached to Stoke Newington police station and who was armed, covered the car park at the rear of the block of flats while other officers went to the front door. 'Everyone,' admitted Baldry, 'was a bit twitchy at the time,' which probably explained why a furtive gluesniffer in the car park suddenly found the business end of a Smith & Wesson Model 10 revolver shoved up his left nostril.

A confidential wanted poster (For Police Eyes Only) for Martin was quickly assembled. Headed 'THIS MAN IS VERY DANGEROUS', it featured two photographs of the subject, one in drag, the other not. 'BE ON YOUR GUARD', the officers were warned. 'HE WILL NOT HESITATE TO SHOOT' and since five of the handguns from the gunsmiths burglary were still unaccounted for, this was a chilling warning. Lastly, 'DO NOT TAKE ANY CHANCES' and this too was prescient advice; it would be a reckless officer who did.

The Chelsea Kitchen restaurant is now situated in the Fulham Road, but at the time of the hunt for Martin, it was sited at the 'smart' end of the King's Road, near Sloane Square. Clive Cox was then a detective constable at Chelsea police station and he received a call from the restaurant to say that Martin was in the premises. He had been recognised by the manager since he had been a regular customer. Cox and other officers were detailed to go to the restaurant and, if necessary, follow Martin until the 'D' Division officers could arrive. Martin emerged from the restaurant; he was followed by a waitress who shook a napkin in his direction to identify him to the police. Martin later told Stephens that he had seen this rather overt signal, plus he was relying on his anti-surveillance instincts so he walked slowly along King's Road, using the shop windows as mirrors and with his hands in his pockets he walked across the road, saw Cox and instantly identified him as being a police officer. There was no sign of the other officers so, as Cox told me, 'At this point I thought I would try to follow him.'

Martin walked into Cheltenham Terrace, a one-way street next to the Duke of York's Territorial Army base headquarters and got into a dark saloon car, correctly parked, facing the King's Road. But then he turned the car around, driving off against the oncoming traffic; Cox flagged down an area car but it was too late. 'I knew he was dangerous,' Cox said. 'He kept two guns, one to hand over, the other to shoot you with.'

Therefore it was decided to keep up observation, and follow Martin's girlfriend. On New Year's Eve, following her return from her parents' home, Superintendent Ness and DS Martin had interviewed Stephens and left her in no doubt that in the event of David Martin contacting her, she should inform them immediately.

According to Stephens, during a three-hour interview she was told, 'You know that if we see him, we're going to have to kill him? This time there can't be any mistakes.' Was that really said? And if it was, was it done, not as a threat of future intentions but to promote a positive, helpful reaction?

What I do know is that I used a ploy, similar to the one allegedly suggested to Stephens, when I was looking for a south London tearaway who had escaped from prison and was allegedly in possession of a firearm with which, he had supposedly stated, he would use on any police officer impertinent enough to try to arrest him. I spent the best part of a week fruitlessly searching for him while spending fairly substantial amounts of the commissioner's budget for information, which prompted the detective inspector to scrawl caustically across the 'expenses' section of my CID diary, 'Try nicking your informant!' Eventually, I confronted the escapee's brother – not the sharpest knife in the drawer – and made a suggestion which caused a look of near-imbecile consternation to appear on his acne-marked face. 'Wot?' he gasped. 'Yew expect me to stick up me own bwuvver?'

'Look at it this way,' I said reasonably. 'Wouldn't it be better for him to give himself up, go back to jail, have a bit more added on to his sentence for breaking out and then, later on, to be released; or for him to meet up with me and have his brains blown out all over the ceiling?'

The pure, inescapable logic of this solution worked. The following day, the escaped prisoner – minus a gun, if indeed one ever existed – surrendered himself to me. Of course, this highly satisfactory state of affairs would not have come about had his sibling been aware that I was not an authorised shot, but I thought it unnecessary to inform him of this pertinent fact.

But even supposing this was said to Stephens, it did not have the desired effect. Keeping observation on her was not a twenty-four hour a day matter; to start with, it was very much an ad hoc affair. There were insufficient staff to carry out full surveillance, plus they had other enquiries to carry out, so the observations were fairly haphazard. At some stage, it seems that a warrant was granted by the Home Secretary to have her telephone calls intercepted; but when Martin telephoned her – using an American accent and the alias 'Pete' – to ask if she would watch the Sylvester Stallone film *First Blood* at the Paris Pullman cinema with him in the Fulham Road on 3 January 1983, and then to dine at Parson's Restaurant thereafter, it appears the police were unaware of it. Afterwards, Martin, who was driving a BMW, dropped her off in Abbey Road and she walked the rest of the way home. Two nights later, they met for a meal at the same restaurant.

On 6 January, the police may not have seen Susie Stephens meet up with Peter Enter, a 26-year-old electrician from St Charles Square, 295 Ladbroke Grove and Lester Kenton Purdy, a 31-year-old film editor of Grovelands Road, Palmers Green. Travelling in two vehicles, one a Ford Capri, the other a hired Mercedes G-Wagen (much needed for its capacity), they made their way to Pickfords in Fulham, where the outstanding charges of £74 were paid, the items stolen by Martin were signed for in the name of 'J. Perry' and the goods were taken to Enter's basement flat.

It was not until the following day that an observation post (OP) was set up in a disused flat, above the NatWest Bank and opposite Stephens's address. However, it may have been set up too late to observe Stephens leaving to carry out a second journey to transport the remainder of Martin's stolen property to Ladbroke Grove. On Monday 10 January, Stephens met Martin at the Odeon Cinema at Swiss Cottage, thence to the ABC Cinema in Fulham to watch Steve Martin in *Dead Men Don't Wear Plaid* and afterwards they went for a meal at a restaurant in Hampstead. If the watchers saw her leave the flat, they may not have known it was her; two other girls lived in the flats and in any event, Stephens would later admit that she wore a black wig, different clothes and high heels, used anti-surveillance techniques and changed tube trains on four or five occasions when she went to meet Martin. On that occasion, Martin – he was then driving a Ford Sierra (of which more later) – dropped her off at Hampstead Tube Station, after they arranged to meet the following night at Swiss Cottage. When Stephens failed to keep the appointment, an irritated Martin telephoned her on Wednesday 12 January and was dismissively told that 'something had come up'.

It was on the day following Martin's aggrieved phone call that Superintendent Ness called a meeting at the incident room. Some of the members of his team were present and they had the added assistance of C11, Scotland Yard's Intelligence Branch.

C11 – it had previously been known as C5(2) Department – had been formed in March 1960. Its aim had been to collate details of all the top criminals (known as 'Main Index' men, including some who had never been arrested) and gather information about them – sightings, car registration numbers, associates – by means of the local collators' offices, via the beat and CID officers on whose ground the criminals lived. In addition, C11 operatives' informants, telephone intercepts, covert OPs, photographs and bugging devices (both in buildings and on vehicles) were utilised in order to collect and disseminate the information to the units most suited to deal with it: the Flying Squad, the Regional Crime Squad or the Drugs Squad. The unit provided Prison Liaison Officers, who reported back details of serious offenders about to be released from prison as well as passing on information gleaned from other prisoners.

C11 seldom carried out arrests themselves; of course, if necessary they could do so, but that was not their specified role, which was a clandestine one. Having carried out their work, they melted back into the shadows. They also possessed a fleet of nondescript vehicles: vans (whose sides often displayed untruthful business logos), cars, taxis and motorcycles. Their surveillance squad which was set up in 1978 was second to none; mainly recruited from the uniform branch[1] they were highly trained, with interchangeable and reversible clothing, and they were unobtrusive, able to neatly fit into the surroundings of an East End pub, as they would be in the American Bar at the Savoy.[2] Other surveillance officers were trained by the Special Air Service as 'rurals': operatives who would climb trees, burrow into the ground and on one auspicious occasion, an officer remained up to his neck in water for forty-eight hours to keep observation on suspects. Needless to say, any police officer who involved C11 in their investigations held them in the highest esteem.

On 12 January, Detective Sergeant Colin Hockaday, who was running the Crime Squad at Paddington Green, was told by Detective Superintendent Ness – who knew that Hockaday had just joined 'D' Division from the Flying Squad and who was an authorised shot – that he was seconding him to join his team in the

---

1. They were given the honorary application of 'detective' to precede their rank; however, they were not CID officers per se.
2. One young female officer, blonde and massively endowed, attended a C11 selection board only to be told, 'Sorry, dear; there's three things against you – and one of them's your hair!'

hunt for Martin. The following day, Thursday 13 January, Hockaday and the other officers, including some from C11s Unit No. 2 Team, attended the briefing at Paddington Green's incident room.

Most of the officers present did not know Martin, including the C11 surveillance team. During the detailed briefing, Superintendent Ness explained that Martin was a transvestite who could pass for a woman and distributed colour photographs of Martin, plus other photographs in the possession of police – in excess of twenty of them, plus nineteen photographs of Stephens. He was described as being aged 35, five feet ten, of slim build with a prominent nose, with long blond hair, blue eyes and crooked teeth who walked with very short, mincing steps, like a woman. Enquiries had revealed Purdy's identity who was believed to have associated with and provided transport for Stephens, plus his photograph and address, together with Enter's address which were passed on to the team. Superintendent Ness emphasised the danger element when dealing with Martin, that he had already shot and wounded a security guard during the course of a robbery and a police officer during the course of a burglary, and stressed that on the last occasion he had been arrested he had had two firearms in his possession and that of the twenty-four guns which had been stolen from the Covent Garden gunsmiths, five were still not accounted for. Therefore, extreme caution had to be exercised at all times. The sighting at The Chelsea Kitchen was mentioned as were other recent sightings where it was stated that Martin had outwitted the police by driving off the wrong way down one-way streets, having no regard whatsoever for the safety of members of the public. It all indicated that he was still in the London area.

The plan was to keep observation on Stephens. She was described as being five foot five, aged 25, slim build with very short hair, the colour of which could change daily, and if this resulted in her meeting Martin, to follow, then 'house' him. It was not the intention to arrest Martin on the street; in the event that Martin was followed to a premises, the authority of the Deputy Assistant Commissioner 'A' Department (Operations) had been sought to deploy D11, the police firearms team, to contain the situation with the intention of peacefully carrying out Martin's arrest. They would not be called in earlier because this would be stretching their resources, plus the fact that (at that time) they were used on static plots, not mobile ones.

However, there was always the possibility that Martin could become aware of the police presence, in which case he might have to be arrested in the open; therefore two of the 'D' Division officers, DC Peter Finch and DS Colin Hockaday, would be armed with Smith & Wesson Model 10 six-shot revolvers. They would also man the OP. In the event that Stephens made off in a vehicle from her address, they would alert C11 by radio and then follow on behind the surveillance team. However, should Martin be spotted, it would be C11 who would be closest to him and therefore they sought authority for two of their officers to be armed as well. This was granted and Detective Constables John Jardine, a 37-year-old Scot and 34-year-old John 'Fred' Deane were also armed, in their case with the handguns issued to Central officers: Smith & Wesson Model 36 five-shot revolvers.

Arming the police had always been a contentious matter. The British police were the envy of the civilised world for going about their duties largely unarmed. However, during the early 1880s two Metropolitan police officers were shot dead and another seriously wounded by burglars, which in 1883 prompted the *Evening Standard* to lead a press campaign to arm the police:

> It is not only foolish but absolutely cruel to send policemen to combat men possessed of revolvers, without any arm, other than a short club. If the law will not protect the police by heavy penalties from armed resistance, they should at least have weapons to enable them to defend their lives.

The superintendents of divisions loftily stated that their men did not wish to be armed; however, the rank and file disagreed and in a poll, 4,430 out of 6,325 officers opted to be armed with revolvers while patrolling night beats in the outer divisions.

The first officer to fire his weapon was Police Constable 161 'P' Henry Owen. On 18 February 1887, he fired all six shots from his Webley 'Metropolitan Police Revolver' into the air to awaken the inhabitants of a burning house in Keston Village after all other means had failed: 'I blew my whistle, lustily called out "Fire!" and hammered at the shutters.' Owen's inspector supported his actions; his superintendent did not. A report was forwarded to one of the two assistant commissioners, Lieutenant-Colonel Richard Pearson, who, three days after the shooting rather dismissively minuted the papers to the commissioner with the words, 'I do not attach much blame to the PC.' Nor most likely did Thomas Cyrus Haslitt, the 87-year-old occupant of the burning house, plus the three other members of his family, who were awoken by the sound of the gunshots, especially after PC Owen assisted in rescuing the contents of the building and extinguishing the blaze, which gutted the premises.

The practice of night duty patrols carrying firearms started to die out in 1893 and following the inadequate weaponry and poor marksmanship displayed by police during the Siege of Sidney Street in 1911, 1,000 .32 Webley & Scott automatic pistols were issued. However, within a short space of time, these became dangerous with many being capable of being fired when the safety catch was on. During the 1930s, a total of nineteen new pistols with 608 rounds of ammunition were issued to each Metropolitan Police division.

During the invasion scare period of the Second World War, the total sum of the armoury allocated to the Flying Squad was a single .32 pistol, kept in a purple case. Its existence was religiously signed for over a period of years before it was discovered that it was unable to fire in any event.

Initially during the post-war years, when the need arose firearms were issued to officers who had some previous experience of them from the armed forces or from gun clubs. Usage of these .38 Webley & Scott revolvers required the officer to fire six shots, with three of them hitting the target. There was, however, no instruction on how the weapon should be loaded. When two police officers were shot dead (and another severely wounded) at West Ham in 1961, firearms were issued to police regardless, to anybody who wanted one, but their knowledge and use of firearms was practically non-existent. One officer loaded his revolver, put it on full cock and simply did not know what to do with it. His colleagues hit the floor while one of their number pluckily shoved a pencil between the gun's hammer and chamber and relieved him of his weapon. Another caused mild panic in the canteen as he brandished his revolver asking anybody who wasn't rushing to get out of the door, 'Where's the safety catch?'

Following the savage murders at Shepherds Bush of the crew of the Q car 'Foxtrot One-one' by Harry Roberts et al. in 1966, there were still few officers who had a clue about weapon handling. One CID officer with a complete disregard for the procreation of a family stuffed a loaded pistol, with the safety catch in the 'off' position, down the front of the waistband of his trousers. But following the Shepherds Bush murders, a firearms unit was formed, known as D11 Branch. Although this was a dedicated unit, training courses were introduced for them to train up divisional and central officers, both uniform and CID. Initially, a four-day course was considered sufficient and divisional officers could, if the need arose, be issued with the Smith & Wesson Model 10 six-shot revolver with a four-inch barrel and for Central CID officers, the more concealable Smith & Wesson Model 36 five-shot revolver with a two-inch barrel. With the abolition of the death penalty, gun crime was on the increase and with it the need for more armed officers.

In 1979, a survey was carried out of all the divisions and branches of the Metropolitan Police to assess how many authorised shots should be trained. It was left to the respective commanders of the twenty-three divisions to determine how many and they arrived at a total figure of 4,601 authorised officers. This was agreed, but by the end of 1979 only 3,820 officers had been trained and when in April the following year a new survey was held to see if the initial figure of 1979 was still a precise one, the commanders now stated that a far more realistic figure was 6,039 authorised shots.

There were simply not enough sites for the officers to be trained and by 1982 complaints that insufficient numbers of officers were being trained were flooding in to D11 Branch. In a review of June that year, D11 complained in turn that they believed that the level of training was insufficient. Ranges were, of course, still required but so was the need for the trainees to practise in realistic surroundings to assess what their actions in dangerous and life-threatening situations should be and D11 suggested a field-craft village be built at the existing training ground at Lippitts Hill. This was ignored and therefore the instructors looked around for temporary accommodation in disused industrial sites which could be utilised. St Olave's Hospital, Bermondsey appeared to fit the bill; by 1979, only forty patients remained and they were transferred to New Cross Hospital and it had partially closed; in fact, it never did re-open and was fully closed in 1985. But the very idea of the disused hospital being used by the police was sufficient for the concept to be denounced by the divisional officer of the public service union, NUPE, who declaimed in the Socialist Worker Party's *News Line*, 'I am appalled to hear there is even the suggestion of the use of the building for a frightening form of police training.'

This then was the level of police firearms training in 1983.

The Follow

The briefing by Detective Superintendent Ness took more than an hour and as Colin Hockaday said, 'It was very full and detailed.' Detective Sergeant Paul Seabrook was in charge of the C11 team; 'In my view,' he said, 'it was a good briefing.' At its conclusion, the briefing was thrown open for discussion and as DC Cyril Jenner said, 'There was ample opportunity for questions and answers, so that everyone present knew their jobs.' For the purposes of the operation, it was decided to refer to Stephens as 'Susie', since the girl with whom she shared the flat was also named Sue; if necessary, the second girl, Susan Sykes, would be referred to either as 'Sue' or 'Tall Sue'.

Hockaday met Peter Finch for the first time at the meeting; his immediate impression of Finch was that he was 'a nice, mild-mannered bloke'. These two officers duly manned the OP to keep observation on Susan Stephens's flat at West End Lane, together with two other officers. Nothing of any importance happened during the observation on that first day; Stephens simply came out of her flat with another girl and went to the Railway public house opposite. She returned at about midnight and in the early hours of the following morning, the observation was terminated.

The following day, Friday 14 January, the operation recommenced at 11.45 a.m. At West Hampstead police station, DS Seabrook briefed four new team members from C11 who had been unable to be present at the initial briefing. He had kept detailed notes from Superintendent Ness's briefing from the previous day and told the team the identities of the armed officers (the same as the previous day) as a safety measure.

This was the disposition of the surveillance team: DS Seabrook with Woman Detective Constable Sharon Collier in a Vauxhall Chevette saloon and DCs Deane and Jardine in an orange Marina van were in the vicinity of Stephens's address; DC Roy Chivers, together with DCs Peter Buddle and Robert Bruce, were in a London taxi; and DCs Ronald White and Cyril Jenner were on solo motorcycles parked at West Hampstead police station. DS Hockaday and DC Finch were again in the OP.

Communications between the various units were on channel seven on the main RT set; these were monitored through Scotland Yard and were recorded. Any discourse between the 'D' Division officers and C11 had to be by means of this medium because only the C11 personnel and their vehicles were fitted with car-to-car radios, operating on channel one, and these were not recorded. However, channel seven was also used by a number of other Central units, Flying Squad and Regional Crime Squad to mention but two, and at that time there was also considerable interference from CB radio enthusiasts. And if that were not enough, in spite of channel one's very limited range, by sheer bad luck another completely separate Central operation on the same channel was being conducted simultaneously nearby.

The officers, including those in the OP, got what appeared to be a strong lead; they had received intelligence that Stephens was going to move to a new address. Since she was in possession of Martin's clothes and belongings, it was reasonable to assume that they would be moving into the new address together. Lester Purdy had been recently escorting Stephens, therefore it was possible that he would provide the transport and details of his green Ford Capri was provided; either that or Stephens would take a London taxi.

At 1.10 p.m., Stephens returned to her flat; in fact, Mr E. Hilton, the owner of 175 West End Lane, had wanted to speak to her but she appeared tense and nervous and replied, 'I can't speak to you now – I'm going to Bath.' At about 4.00 p.m., the officers in the OP saw Purdy's apple-green Ford Capri arrive, which parked opposite to Stephens's flat and two men got out and entered the building.

It was at this stage that problems were experienced in the OP. The portable RT set could receive but not properly transmit (this was a common failing) and a new one had to be acquired and brought in to the OP as quickly and as unobtrusively as possible. Therefore C11 foot units, using their own covert radios, had to be deployed to provide up-to-the-minute reports and then when the new RT set arrived, information from both the main set and the covert radios were transmitted simultaneously; until this was sorted out, it added to the confusion.

Thirty-five minutes later, Stephens, wearing a fur coat, and three men – the third man had remained in the Capri – went into a fruit shop. Ten minutes after that, Stephens put a bag or a suitcase into the back of the Capri, and she and the three men got into the car and drove off. By now, the sun had set and the officers in the OP alerted C11 who immediately started following the vehicle and Hockaday and Finch left the OP, got into Finch's authorised private car – call sign 'Delta 13' and fitted with a main RT set only – and followed the C11 operatives. Right at the end of the tail was Superintendent Ness and DS Tom Martin (the fifth officer to be armed) in a Hillman, call sign 'Delta 56'. Although, like 'Delta 13', this vehicle was not fitted with a small set, Ness's presence was necessary because if Martin were to be picked up and the vehicles were to leave the Metropolitan Police District it would be necessary to contact the constabulary area they had entered in order for that force to provide armed back-up.

The Capri drove down West End Lane, into Abbey Road and into Grove End Road. As the Capri turned right into St John's Wood Road, so the surveillance vehicles followed and travelled down to the junction with Maida Vale where they were held at the lights. They turned right into Maida Vale, then almost immediately left into Clifton Road and into Clifton Gardens. The Capri turned left into Warwick Avenue and reached the roundabout where it turned right on to the Harrow Road underneath the A40(M) flyover. The surveillance vehicles, often changing places, always unobtrusive, followed the target vehicle on to Lord Hill's Bridge where it turned left and took the first right into Westbourne Park Villas, which ran into Westbourne Park Road.

As Hockaday reached the area of Notting Hill, he heard one of the C11 officers say on the radio, 'They're in a different vehicle.' They were. At 4.57 p.m., the Capri had stopped in Kensington Park Road, close to the junction with Westbourne Park Road. WDC Collier got out on foot, strolled towards the Capri and walked up the outside staircase of a block of flats in order to keep observation on the vehicle; DC Deane, meanwhile, was keeping observation from a bus stop, behind the Capri. Stephens and Purdy had gone into the Portobello Mini Hire Ltd at 317 Westbourne Park Road, W11 and as Seabrook would later say, 'There was a lot of coming and going.' Stephens later went into a branch of Bodyshop and at 5.30 p.m., the Capri left; it was driven by Peter Enter, who had been the third man in the car. The other man, a friend of Purdy's named Lewis Muslin, left on foot – he would play no part in the subsequent events.

Some six or seven minutes later, a yellow Mini, registration number GYF 117W, was driven from around the corner by a man not known to the surveillance team. Wearing a bomber jacket, he was slim with long fair hair; he got out, Purdy got into the driver's seat, Stephens got into the back of the car and lay down and the unknown man, into the front passenger seat, and the car drove off.

Seabrook alerted the rest of the team and in the darkness, the Mini was followed by the surveillance vehicles, the motorcycles, taxi, van and cars. Upon being asked by Seabrook – driving the Vauxhall Chevette saloon, call sign 'Central 411' – who the passenger in the Mini was, WDC Collier in the front passenger seat replied, 'I don't know where he came from, but he's very slim and has similar hair to Martin.' Seabrook asked the opinion of other members of the team and DC Chivers, driving a black London taxi, call sign 'Central 422', replied, 'He doesn't look to be five feet ten to me.'

The Mini drove along Ladbroke Grove and into Holland Park Avenue and threaded its way through London's home-going traffic, followed unobtrusively by the surveillance team. As it reached the Shepherd's Bush roundabout, WDC Collier asked DC Deane for a repeat of a message he had transmitted previously about the passenger's nose and hair. 'The nose is a good likeness and so is the hair,' replied Deane, 'especially in the photograph of him dressed as a woman.' Seabrook asked if Deane could confirm whether or not this was a positive identification; Deane, in the orange Marina van, call sign 'Central 415', driven by Jardine, replied, 'Not.'

The Mini turned left into Holland Road, towards Earls Court which was where the Boat Show was being held and the traffic was exceptionally heavy. It turned east into Pembroke Road, a one-way street with three lanes of traffic and as it approached the junction with Earls Court Road, behind a lorry, traffic came to a standstill.

Seabrook informed Ness on the radio, 'He may, I stress, *may* be the wanted man' and Ness replied, 'Received, mind how you go.' Hockaday told Seabrook, 'Received, we'll stay behind you for now,' and Ness told the crew of 'Delta 13', 'Stay back, stay back, leave it to the Central units, over,' but shortly afterwards Ness called Seabrook, saying, 'The only way to resolve it is for one of the crew of 'Delta 13' who know him, to look, over.' This had to be Finch; he was the only officer present who could make a positive identification, since the other officers had to rely purely on photographs.

This transmission was received and then Ness said, '411, we'll wait for a suitable opportunity and maybe in heavy traffic is the best time, over.' There was discussion over the radio as to the location of the Mini and Seabrook said, 'Now's as good a time as any, one of you, I suggest – as soon as they see the white Volkswagen van towing a generator, it's the target vehicle immediately in front of it, over.' The CB interference was worse than ever, and Hockaday replied, 'Received, has he got through the lights?' Seabrook replied that the pedestrians were moving faster than the cars.

The vehicle containing Finch and Hockaday was probably 100 to 150 yards behind the Mini and the other watchers heard the transmission from Hockaday, 'Peter's going on foot, Peter's going on foot, to look at the car', and these messages were often repeated, in case the first words were lost in transmission. 'Tell him to be very careful, we don't want to alarm our man, over,' radioed Ness.

At that moment, as Seabrook had said, the Mini was in front of a Volkswagen van towing a trailer with machinery on board, which Seabrook was using as 'cover'; the three vehicles were on the nearside of the road. Seabrook passed the position of the vehicles but then cancelled the transmission because the traffic began to move. Seconds later, the traffic stopped once more with the vehicles in the same formation. The van, containing Jardine and Deane, was behind Seabrook's Chevette.

To confuse matters in an already tense situation, these were the transmissions being broadcast on channel seven at that time:

Yeah, thousand unit from seven, ten seven one, over.

... ended up being R5 and started off being R2, MP over ...

(Unintelligible)

Yeah, very intermittent now, acknowledged, MP out.

Ten seven one from ten eight five, receiving, over.

Ten eight five from ten seven one, we're in Brixton Road – er – can you give us? (interference).

Seven one, ten seven one, there's Gough Brothers off-licence (interference).

Yeah, ten eight five from ten seven one, you broke up completely, can you repeat please, over.

(Interference)

... seven, MP over.

... sierra five seven five seven from six, are you receiving, six, over.

(Interference)

Seven from six – er – are you returning to five zero, six, over.

Yeah, six from five seven, yes, yes, yes, over.

Can you give me your ETA, please, thanks a lot.

... from five seven, do you receive that, over.

... seven from ... over.

One five minutes, fifteen minutes, over.

Received, six, out.

The person has made off with no money and he was hit back, so he may be injured, over.

It was therefore amazing that any coherent messages got through to anybody, whether connected with the hunt for Martin or not.

However, a chain of events had already been set in motion which would result in tragedy. As the seventeeth-century poet James Shirley said, 'There is no armour against fate,' because at precisely 5.57 p.m. and ten seconds, Finch was now on foot in Pembroke Road, approaching the Mini, gun in hand.

seats and was halfway out of the driver's door. Jardine saw him fumbling with his clothing – this was also witnessed by DC Buddle – and in that split-second, Jardine not only deduced that the man was Martin but also knowing how Martin had previously had a back-up weapon, believed that he was reaching for a gun and he too opened fire three times, hitting him twice. One bullet lodged in his armpit, the other was found on the casualty trolley on admission to hospital.

DC Finch had moved round to the offside of the car and remembering how Martin had previously fiercely struggled, even after being shot when he had been in possession of a back-up weapon, now believed that he was still under threat and pistol-whipped the passenger, several times, fracturing his skull and also the bones in the back of one hand as he instinctively raised it to protect his head.

DC Jenner handcuffed the man and dragged him by his arms from the car, as was Stephens, who was screaming and protesting. A police officer shouted, 'Where are the guns?' Stephens was handcuffed by DC Bruce and searched by WDC Collier, to whom she said, 'What have you done? That wasn't your man!' Fourteen shots had been fired; six had hit the young man and had grievously wounded him.

Hockaday heard the shots, followed by Seabrook on the radio: 'Shots being fired – shots being fired!' He quickly made his way to the Mini where he saw Jardine on the pavement holding Stephens and passed his handcuffs to him; someone shouted, 'One of them's away!' That was Purdy.

It was at that moment that Detective Superintendent Ness arrived; looking down at the young man, half in and half out of the Mini, he said, 'Who is this guy, Colin?'

'I dunno, Guv'nor,' replied Hockaday and not only did he not know the identity of the injured man, neither did anybody else.

It became suddenly and sickeningly clear that the wounded man was not David Martin; it was a 26-year-old freelance film director named Steven Richard Waldorf.

What happened next is best described by John Deane in his statement to the investigation:

> At this point, I still believed that we had detained Martin who had been exchanging shots with DC Finch. As soon as I knew that Waldorf had been restrained with handcuffs, I felt that it was safe to re-holster my gun, which I did. I felt relief that the matter had been concluded without injury to ourselves or any other member of the public. Still believing that we had detained Martin, I turned to DC Finch who said, 'You know it's not him?' I could not believe this as I had been convinced that DC Finch had been exchanging shots with the person believed to be Martin. My initial reaction to his comment was that he was suffering from shock as a result of the incident. I asked him what he meant and he said, 'I'm sorry, it's not him.' I still was not prepared to accept what he was saying so I said to him, 'Are you a hundred per-cent sure, Peter?' He replied, 'Yes, I'm sorry, it's definitely not him.'

It was this realisation that the wrong man had been shot which had undoubtedly prompted the exclamation, 'Oh, fuck!' which was overheard on the Flying Squad's car-to-car radio by Tony Freeman, as he waited for me, several miles away.

Colin Black, one of the team who had been responsible for Martin's arrest ten years earlier, was interviewing a victim of crime in the front office of Kensington police station when a member of the public came in, saying that someone had been shot. 'I went straight to the scene and found out that it was apparently David Martin who had been shot,' recalled Black. 'Everyone was very elated, well, for a short time, until it soon became apparent that it wasn't him.'

Brian Baister QPM, MA was the chief superintendent at Kensington police station; hearing from Detective Superintendent Mike McAdam that there had been a shooting nearby, he dashed out of the police station into Earl's Court Road and ran the 300 yards down to the scene of the incident. 'My intention was to tape off the area, away from the press,' he told me. 'The paparazzi were just round the corner from the shooting, having staked out an apartment where Prince Andrew was a frequent visitor to the home of Koo Stark. When I got there, there was Waldorf hanging half way out of the car; but my fears were groundless; the paparazzi were far more interested in what Prince Andrew was up to and they never showed up!' This was but a moment's light relief in a desperate situation because in Pembroke Road the scene was one of pandemonium.

Detective Constable Andy Muth arrived and turned off the Mini's still-running engine. The first independent senior CID officer to arrive at the scene was Detective Chief Inspector Bob Chapman from Kensington police station. He ensured that the scene was taped off, all unauthorised persons were kept out of the area, floodlighting from Traffic Division had been sent for and now he was awaiting the arrival of the support units. Chapman saw that Waldorf was laying face down in the roadway, bleeding from the back of his head and as he was turned over, a bullet fell from his body. 'His face resembled, in my view quite markedly, the man Martin whom I knew was wanted and whose issued photograph I had seen,' said Chapman. This belief was shared by Detective Sergeant Roger Driscoll who had also hurried there from Kensington police station. 'I saw the PCs turn him over and then saw his face,' he said. 'In my opinion, it was the man called David Martin whose picture I had seen on various appeal posters.' Driscoll was then deputed to become the exhibits officer in the case.

The handcuffs were removed from Waldorf but Police Constable 342 'B' Timothy Davis held on to his left arm, in case he attempted any violent movements because he heard someone at the scene say, 'That's the bloke from Marlborough Street.' PC Davis said, 'From that, I assumed that the victim was the man Martin, wanted for attempted murder and escaping from custody.'

A woman who told police she was a nurse arrived – this was Jane Lamprill – with some dressings. Police Constable 166 'B' Adrian Dwyer heard Waldorf moaning several times, 'God help me, God help me.'

Baroness Helen de Westenholz had witnessed some of the incident from her home, which overlooked the scene. 'Whilst I was watching, I heard one or two more gunshot cracks but I couldn't actually see where they came from,' she said. 'Then I saw that the driver [*sic*] of the Mini had sort of fallen out of his car, he was hanging out from the waist up on to the road with his head on the floor.'

George Edward Carter had been the driver of the Volkswagen van towing the jetting unit and as he pulled up behind the Mini, his dipped headlights illuminated the car and he could see there were three occupants: the back seat passenger was a girl, sitting on the nearside. Carter saw Finch approach the car but his recollection was that one shot was fired whereupon 'the Mini began to go down on the nearside' and that he then moved to the back of the Mini, fired two shots through the back window, then returned to the car's nearside and fired one shot through the passenger's window. He then saw a man trying to get through the driver's window and when Carter got out of his van and moved back, he heard another report, followed by four more. He described seeing a man, holding a gun by the nearside of the Mini who shouted, 'There's a girl in the back, shall I get her out?' and the girl got out of the car via the passenger door and complained of an injury to her back.

And then Carter stated that more men appeared, one of whom had a card in his breast pocket – this appeared to be a police warrant card – and the man who had carried out the initial shooting said to him, 'I put one in the tyre and noticed movement in the car so I put two through the back window.' The man with the card – and it is possible this was Detective Sergeant Tom Martin – replied either, 'You did good,' or 'You did well.'

David Eric Still was Carter's brother-in-law and he was a passenger in the Volkswagen van. Initially, he noticed that there was a girl in the back of the Mini and his attention was drawn to her because on several occasions, she had looked out of the Mini's rear window and had then laid down 'out of sight'. Of the two men occupying the front seats in the Mini, Still initially thought that the front seat passenger was a girl, 'because the person had long hair to the shoulders'. Still concurred with Carter about the initial shooting but then said that the gunman had moved round behind the Mini, in front of the van, to the offside of the Mini and saw a second man, holding a gun and pointing it into the Mini's open passenger door. Still then heard three more shots and believed that they were fired by the man who had initially fired and then Still knelt down between the driver's and passenger's seats in the van while his brother-in-law got out. When he got up, he saw a man lying half out of the Mini's driver's door – his feet were still inside the car – and saw a man crouched over the body and hit him, twice over the head, with a gun. The man from the Mini was handcuffed and then Still saw the girl whom he had originally seen in the back of the

Mini in the road. A woman was searching her, and the girl who was crying was saying, 'But it's not him, it's not him.' Still too heard the comment 'You done well' and then he and Carter both described how they were approached by a young uniformed officer who told both of them to 'Fuck off'. Nobody admitted to making *that* remark. The incident had certainly unnerved both Carter and Still; when they volunteered their testimony to the police the following day they did so in the presence of a solicitor and requested copies of their statements.

Mrs Mavis Connell was driving her dark blue Saab saloon along Pembroke Road with Samuel Fleming as her front seat passenger. The windows as well as the sunshine roof were all half open because both of them were smoking. Mrs Connell was in the offside lane, the middle lane was clear and in the nearside lane she saw a yellow Mini and drew up parallel to it; her view was quite uninterrupted. Traffic was at a standstill and Mrs Connell turned to speak to her passenger when she suddenly saw two men appear from the nearside of the Volkswagen van parked behind the Mini. Both men were pointing guns at the Mini; she heard what she thought were two shots and saw that the Mini's passenger door window had crazed. Almost immediately, she saw four or five other men, all of whom appeared to be holding guns run up to the Mini from behind. She heard two shots fired and believed these to have come from the running men and she saw the Mini's rear window craze over. One gunman she saw pointing his gun at the driver's door and heard several more shots fired; she could see two people in the front of the Mini who were cowering down. Almost immediately, the driver's door opened and the driver ran off and the Mini moved forwards a few yards, so that she could see the rear number plate, which she partly, inaccurately, recalled as being 'CYF'. At the same time, the man who had been firing was reloading his gun.

Mrs Connell saw the Mini's passenger emerge from the driver's door, holding his bloodied head in his hands and collapse into the road. The gunman nearest to Mrs Connell shouted, 'Don't move!' to the man in the road and as a pedestrian emerged from in front of her car, the same man shouted, 'Get back, we're police.'

'This,' said Mrs Connell, 'was the first time I heard the word "police" mentioned.'

She could hear a girl screaming – this of course was Stephens – and the gunman plus a man in motorcycle gear (this was DC Jenner) pulled the wounded man out of the Mini, on to the roadway and handcuffed him.

Mrs Connell's passenger, Samuel Kenneth Fleming, heard two cracks, although at the time he did not immediately identify them as gunshots. Looking to his left, he saw a man pointing a gun at a yellow Mini, saw there were three people inside it and then heard the sound of several more shots. Initially, Fleming got the impression that blanks were being fired because he did not see a barrel flash or any of the weapons 'kick'. Several more men ran towards the Mini and Fleming heard a number of other shots discharged; he saw one man by the Mini's rear offside reloading his revolver. At that moment, the driver's door opened, a man ran off, the car rolled forward a few feet and then more shooting came from the rear of the Mini. A man scrambled across the driver's seat and then collapsed into the roadway and Fleming saw a motorcyclist handcuff the man.

'The traffic started moving and before our way ahead was clear, we were peremptorily instructed to move on,' said Fleming, adding 'or words to that effect'. This may or may not have been a tactful way of echoing the less than tactful police officer's words heard by the occupants of the Volkswagen van.

The traffic in Pembroke Road had been travelling so slowly that Keith Victor Daniels turned off the engine of his Hillman

Hunter saloon which was in that thoroughfare's offside lane. He was about thirty yards from the junction with Earls Court Road when he heard a bang, followed seconds later by several more. He looked across the road, at an angle of forty-five degrees, saw a yellow Mini and over the top of it, a man by the nearside door. He was unable to see the man's arms but then heard the sound of more bangs and saw the rear window of the Mini shatter. Daniels saw the driver run out, across the road and then saw two men with guns go to the Mini's offside. One of the men reloaded his gun and both men pointed their weapons at a man who was sprawling out of the open driver's door and then Daniels believed he saw one of the men hit the man in the roadway with his gun, anything between two to four times; at the time, the man had both hands on top of his head. Before he drove on, Daniels saw a woman in a brown cape who ran to the scene, spoke briefly to a motorcyclist and then ran back in the direction from which she had come.

This was Jane Rosemary Lamprill, a secretary for the Press Association and also a trained state registered nurse. From her flat in Pembroke Road, she heard the sound of shots; she looked out into the street but all she could see was a traffic jam. She ran out into the street, saw the Mini and a man holding a gun, heard that someone had been shot, ran back to her flat and telephoned the police, ambulance and her employers. She returned to the scene, carrying first-aid materials and saw a man, obviously injured, lying in the road. By now, he was no longer handcuffed and a number of uniformed officers were in attendance. She felt his pulse, checked that he was breathing and tried to ascertain the extent of his injuries. Lamprill saw that he was losing blood from the right side of his temple and the back of his head, so she applied packs to the head injuries and bandaged it. A police officer opened part of the man's clothing and she could see a lot of blood; she also saw the police officer pick up a bullet from the man's shirt near a chest wound, so she placed a bandage as a pack over the wound to prevent both air getting in and blood coming out. Lamprill suspected, quite rightly, that there was liver damage. An ambulance arrived and she accompanied the man, whom she described as being aged about 30, slight to medium build, shoulder-length fairish hair with blue eyes, to St Stephen's Hospital. She comforted him and heard him saying, 'It hurts.' Also in the ambulance was Stephens who appeared to be in pain and was agitated.

One odd point: Lamprill had spoken to DS Tom Martin at length but when she asked for his details, he appeared reluctant to give them and told her, 'I don't want to get involved.' It was a strange thing to say, because Martin quite definitely was involved and furthermore, Stephens would later say that following the shooting, Martin came round the car to her and when she asked, 'Why? Why?' he allegedly replied, 'I don't know, we are all frightened.'

Lamprill also told police that in her opinion, the photograph of David Martin shown on the front page of the *Daily Express* dated Saturday 15 January 1983 bore a likeness to the man she had treated. However, she also stated that the photograph of Steven Waldorf published in the same newspaper three days later bore 'little resemblance to the man I attended in the street at the time of the shooting on 14 January 1983'.

Undeniably, most of the witnesses' testimony was slightly confused and contradictory, quite normal and understandable given the shocking circumstances of the incident. One witness said that she had not seen any brutality by the police; indeed, she stated, they were 'quite gentle' and this was backed up by another bystander. Another witness said he saw two men running away from the car and yet another said that the shots had been fired by motorcyclists. A woman stated that she saw the shots fired; then in a follow-up statement said that she didn't and another was sure that the police were carrying rifles.

Although Finch asserted that he had shouted 'Armed Police!' (and perhaps he had, or truly believed that he had), nobody – police or any of the eighty-three members of the public who lived in, or were in, the area who had been interviewed by the investigators – had heard a warning given.

The Investigation

B oth Waldorf and Stephens were taken to St Stephen's Hospital in the Fulham Road, Chelsea. Stephens, who believed she had been hit in the back by a bullet, was seen by Dr Pauline Ann Cutting at 6.24 p.m. She had a bruise measuring three by one-and-a-half inches on the lower back of her chest with an abrasion half that size over the left lower ribs posteriorly. There were no other apparent injuries and to exclude any underlying injuries or the presence of 'any foreign body', X-rays of her chest and abdomen were taken, the wound was cleaned and dressed, she was given an antitetanus toxoid booster injection and was discharged. In fact, one of the bullets fired by Deane – it was later found lodged in the back of the Mini's front passenger seat – had scraped across Stephens's fur coat (fibres from the coat were found on the bullet) and it was this which had caused the abrasion on her back. After questioning at Kensington police station, at 5 a.m. she was taken home to her flat by a female police officer.

Waldorf was, of course, a different matter. Six bullets had entered his body and when his blood-soaked clothes were cut off him they revealed – including entry and exit holes – a total of eleven bullet holes in his clothing. At just over one-and-a-half inches long, the .38 Special ammunition that had been fired from the police revolvers were low pressure cartridges which travelled at rather low speeds; their maximum firing range was fifty yards.

However, from the distance they had been fired at Waldorf – practically at point-blank range – they had caused appalling damage and his life now hung in the balance.

Peter Opie, the Senior House Officer, was in the hospital's accident and emergency department when he received a phone call informing him of an approaching patient suffering from gunshot wounds. Waldorf was brought into the resuscitation area; he was conscious but moaning with pain. Mr Opie commenced an intravenous infusion in his arm and the nurses started to cut away the blood-soaked clothing. He noted that Waldorf's pulse rate was ninety-two and that his systolic blood pressure was found to have ninety millimetres of mercury. There were two small cuts, one on his right temple and another on his upper right abdomen, over the liver. On his right and left shoulders were bullet wounds, two in each shoulder, front and back, and also two in his left thigh, some of which contained pieces of clothing and another bullet lodged over the left lung. Radiographical examination commenced and films were taken of the chest and skull. There was a depressed fracture on the right-hand side of the skull and Mr Opie initially guessed, incorrectly, that this might have been caused by a ricocheting bullet. Waldorf's right hand was swollen with two small cuts to the back of the hand and the third metacarpal bone was fractured at its base. As Waldorf was turned on his right-hand side, a bullet was discovered from the wound in his clothing. By the time he was taken to the operating theatre, his blood pressure had increased to 120.

The surgeon who next saw Waldorf was Nasser Ahmed Nasser. Although Mr Opie had intravenously administered five milligrams of diamorphine, Mr Nasser noticed that nevertheless Waldorf was crying out in pain. He immediately informed Ronald Hoile, the Senior Surgical Registrar, who subsequently met Mr Nasser in the operating theatre.

Waldorf was prepared for an exploratory operation and surgery commenced at 8.10 p.m. Mr Hoile was the surgeon and he was assisted by Mr Nasser and two other surgeons and three anaesthetists were also in attendance. In addition to the other injuries, a wound was found at the back of the right armpit, measuring two centimetres. The exploration of the abdomen revealed that the bullet had shattered the eighth and ninth ribs, had penetrated the right lobe of the liver and initially appeared to be lost in the diaphragm; however, that bullet had already been recovered at the scene. There was a large ragged cavity in the liver, which was just missing the inferior vena cava – the veins that convey blood to the heart – but the tissue destruction was extensive because of the profuse bleeding. Therefore, the cavity in the liver was temporarily packed to stop the bleeding, the vessels involved were tied off and the right lobe of the liver was cut back and the edge was stitched. The abdomen was closed with drainage and a chest drain was inserted on the right. Bullets from his shoulders were removed and those wounds, together with those in the left thigh, right flank and temple, were excised. Waldorf had lost five litres of blood and nineteen units of blood were transfused.

Over the next forty-eight hours, Waldorf's condition stabilised. However, by 7.30 p.m. on Sunday 16 January it became obvious that he was bleeding intra-abdominally and he was taken back to the operating theatre. The inferior vena cava had in fact ruptured, probably due to the contusion of the bullet which had caused the liver injury, and once more there was profuse bleeding. Thankfully, during the ninety-minute operation, the vena cava was able to be repaired, but the following morning staff in the intensive care unit discovered that one of Waldorf's lungs, punctured by a bullet, had filled with blood. This was swiftly dealt with and his condition, once again stable though still critical, gradually started to improve and he was transferred to the intensive therapy unit.

When the consultant forensic pathologist Iain Eric West examined both Waldorf and his X-rays on Friday 28 January, he came to the conclusion that the skull fracture had not occurred as the result of a bullet wound or a fall on to flat ground. He believed that it was consistent with a blow from a hard object which could have been caused by the frame or cylinder of a revolver. Similarly, the fracture to the metacarpal he believed to have been caused by being struck on the back of the hand with considerable force, on probably two occasions by 'an object of limited striking area'.

It was thanks to the brilliance of Ronald Hoile and his team at St Stephen's Hospital – and quite possibly the prompt action of Jane Lamprill at the scene – that Steven Waldorf's life was saved.

Back at the scene of the shooting, witnesses were being spoken to and the area was being meticulously searched for spent bullets, cartridge cases and any other items of interest; uniformed police officers assisted in the search, scenes-of-crime officers bagged up exhibits and in the early hours of Saturday morning, the yellow Mini was loaded on to a trailer. It was then conveyed to the Metropolitan Police Forensic Science Laboratory at 109 Lambeth Road, Lambeth where it was placed in an examination room, and the room locked.

Meanwhile, the three traumatised detectives had been taken to Kensington police station by Detective Constable Stephen Hoile. 'They appeared to me to be very dazed and obviously suffering from severe shock,' he said. 'They looked so bad I asked them whether they wanted to see a doctor. None of them replied. They were so dazed I don't think what I said registered with them.'

This was undoubtedly correct. 'At this point, I still felt from what happened that it might be Martin and that DC Finch might be mistaken,' said Deane. 'I felt very shocked by the whole incident.'

The officers were immediately debriefed by the commander of 'B' District, Robert Innes; Chief Superintendent Baister took possession of the officers' weapons and remaining ammunition until they were packaged by a scenes-of-crime officer.

DCI Chapman had now returned to Kensington police station where he saw the three officers, together with DS Seabrook, in the chief superintendent's office. To all of them, he said, 'I am not the investigating officer for this matter, nor am I likely to be. I am the detective chief inspector of Kensington police station but until the appointment of and arrival of an investigating officer, I am assuming control of the scene. For that purpose, I will require to know, briefly, in which direction bullets were fired.' To DS Seabrook he asked, 'Can you tell me about it?' Although Seabrook was able to furnish brief details of the static and mobile observations, he was unable to assist as to the direction of gunfire.

Chapman then said to Finch, 'I'll have to ask you where you fired your gun. That is all I want.'

Finch replied, 'I fired my first two shots into the rear tyre.'

'Is that the nearside tyre?' asked Chapman and Finch replied, 'Yes.'

'Did you fire any more?' asked Chapman.

'Yes,' Finch replied. 'Then I fired another four through the front passenger window into his arm and I saw them go into his arm.' Finch then rubbed his left upper arm and shoulder to indicate where his bullets had gone.

At some point, Finch mentioned hitting Waldorf over the head with his gun but he did not expand on that subject and Chapman – who only wanted to know about the number and trajectory of the bullets – did not question him further, only asking, 'Were they in a downward direction?' and Finch replied, 'Yes.'

Chapman then asked Deane, 'Where did you fire yours?'

He replied, 'I was behind the car and fired all five into the rear window.'

'There only appears to be four holes in the rear window,' said Chapman and Deane replied, 'Our guns only have five rounds but I'm sure all five went into the back window.'

'Were they in a downward direction?' asked Chapman and was told, 'Reasonably, yes.'

To Jardine, Chapman said, 'What about yours?'

He replied, 'I fired three at him when he was halfway out of the car and halfway on the road.'

'Did you see where they went?' asked Chapman and Jardine replied, 'They hit him.'

'Then I assume they were all in a downward direction?' queried Chapman and was told, 'Yes.'

The three officers were taken to the police station's canteen where they were kept segregated until the arrival of the investigating officers from the Police Complaints Branch, CIB2. And while this was going on, precisely what had happened was being pieced together. The questions that needed answers were: why were the three people in the Mini, why had it been hired and where was it going?

Susan Stephens made two statements to police, the first on the day following the shooting, the second five days later to clear up any ambiguities contained in the first, in the presence of a solicitor. She simply said that she was waiting for Lester Purdy to pick her up at her flat; exactly why was never made clear.

Lester Kenton Purdy made three statements; the first on the day following the shooting was written by Commander Taylor. The two subsequent statements were made on 24 January in the presence of his solicitor, Arwyn Hopkins (he would later act for Steven Waldorf in his civil proceedings against the police) of Pelleys Solicitors. Purdy stated that he had been in a relationship with Marion, the sister of Steven Waldorf, for some three-and-a-half years. He and Steven were good friends who occasionally worked together in the film business. On 14 January, he had arranged to meet Waldorf at a car hire company; they intended to go to Coulsdon to pick up a Toyota for use in a film shoot. Before the meet with Waldorf, Purdy had gone to Stephens's address in his Capri because she wanted to come along 'for the ride'.

Waldorf's statement was not obtained until 27 January when it was taken down by Detective Chief Superintendent Dickens. Waldorf stated that he had met Stephens in December 1982 and had met her thereafter on about five occasions. Both Purdy and Waldorf said that they knew the name of David Martin, because he had been a friend of Susie Stephens; however, both stated that they had never met or spoken to him. Waldorf had known Peter Enter, a friend of Lester Purdy's, since 1979 and when in late October 1982, Waldorf had started working for a film director named Tony Palmer who lived in Kensington Park Gardens, he decided that he needed a flat nearer to the area than his parents' home at Arkley, Barnet. He had heard of a flat becoming available at 295 Ladbroke Grove and because the letting agents would only agree to the flat being 'company let', Purdy arranged the tenancy through his company Beachshore Ltd, with Waldorf as the tenant. In the event, he stayed there for not more than a total of five nights. Peter Enter moved into the small bedroom of the flat and when Stephens arranged, via Purdy, to move into the flat as well – she was not, as Waldorf understood it, getting on with her flat mate at West End Lane – she would start paying Waldorf's share of the rent. However, although she had moved some of her belongings into the flat, he was unaware if she had commenced paying any rent.

Peter Enter had arrived at Stephens's flat; according to Purdy 'he had nothing else to do' and he too got into the Capri and at the car hire company, he drove off in the Capri. Both Stephens and Purdy stated that it was Enter's intention to go to Box, a village outside Bath, to see Hugh Cornwell, a member of the band The Stranglers, regarding completing the wiring at a studio before returning the Capri to Purdy's address.

At the car hire company, Purdy stated that Waldorf had forgotten his driving licence and chequebook, so he paid for the hire of the Mini. The car hire's company secretary, Mrs Teresa Walley, who arranged the hire, recalled that Purdy said that he was in a hurry to get to Coulsdon and while he was at the counter he was studying an $A–Z$. The three – Purdy, Stephens and Waldorf – got into the hired yellow Mini and drove off. From time to time, Stephens would lie down on the back seat because, as she would later tell the investigating officers, 'she felt tired'.

Stationary in Pembroke Road, Waldorf turned to speak to Purdy and Stephens when Purdy saw a man holding a gun by the passenger's door and heard two loud bangs. No bullets entered the car – these, of course, were the shots going into the rear nearside tyre – and as Purdy later said, 'I thought for a moment that it might be someone fooling around with a starting pistol.' Waldorf too had heard what he described as being 'two or three softish sounding bangs'.

More shots were fired, these into the car; Waldorf was hit, Stephens screamed 'Lester!' Purdy shouted 'Leg it!', and ran but later turned back to see Waldorf being pulled out of the car. Meanwhile, Stephens had been trying to get down on the floor because there was a weight – Waldorf – on the driver's seat which she was unable to push forward. 'I felt something hit me in the back,' she said, 'as if I had been hit with a cricket bat.'

The police, said Stephens believed they had shot David Martin, upon which she screamed, 'Go and look at his fucking face!'

As she and Waldorf were later conveyed to hospital, she could hear him murmuring, 'My God, it hurts, it hurts.'

Although Brian Arnold, a principal scientific officer attached to the laboratory, had already made an examination of the vehicle at the scene, in the days that followed he made a further detailed examination of the Mini at the Metropolitan Police Forensic Science Laboratory and took possession of various items of clothing, spent bullets and fragments of bullets. He test-fired the three detectives' revolvers and found they were all in good condition. All six chambers of Finch's weapon had been fired, as had three chambers of Jardine's weapon and in the case of Deane's weapon, all five chambers had been fired.

Arnold examined one item which was thought to be part of a bullet; however, it was not. Of the fourteen remaining items, two exhibits which were described as bullets and which had been found in the roadway were in fact bullet fragments. A bullet that Arnold had extracted from the driver's door was very badly damaged and like the previous two items lacked characteristic detail.

A microscopic examination was made by comparing bullets that Arnold had fired from the detective's revolvers and the last eleven spent bullets, which showed varying degrees of damage and several of which revealed evidence of impact with glass and/or clothing. He came to these conclusions:

> Finch's gun had fired bullets which were found on the floor of the Mini, in the front passenger footwell, the rear nearside wheel arch and the back of Waldorf's left shoulder. There were also indications that that gun had fired bullets one of which emerged from Waldorf when he was lying on the offside of the Mini and also a flattened bullet found in the roadway.
>
> Jardine had fired bullets, one of which was extracted from Waldorf's left armpit at the hospital and a second which was found under Waldorf's body, also at the hospital.
>
> Lastly, one of the bullets fired from Deane's gun was lodged in the interior of the front passenger seat, another had fallen from Waldorf's clothing and the third had been extracted from Waldorf's right armpit at the hospital.

The pieces of the metaphorical jigsaw were slowly coming together. The independent witnesses had said what they had seen. The exhibits had been – and were being still – scrupulously gathered and recorded. The scene had been photographed and plans of the area drawn up. All the evidence was being marshalled together. Now it would be the turn of the detectives who had fired the shots to explain what had happened; and what they had to say would be crucial.

Enter the Complaints
Department – CIB2

Up to and including the early 1970s, there were corrupt practices in the Metropolitan Police. Corruption was not endemic in the ranks of the CID but there existed a small cadre of deeply crooked CID officers and their activities badly needed to be addressed, dealt with and eradicated. No honest cop was in any doubt about that. Unfortunately, the person deputed to deal with this dissolute behaviour was the new commissioner, Sir Robert Mark GBE, QPM. Not only did he possess a vitriolic hatred of the CID, he was also utterly determined to break their power. To this end, he formed the police complaints department, which was then known as A10. A senior uniform officer was in charge and the investigating officers were drawn from the uniform and CID branches.

Mark may have disliked introducing those despised CID officers into his anti-corruption unit but the fact remained that they were necessary, because few of their uniform counterparts possessed any investigatory skills or the ability to compose a coherent report to the Director of Public Prosecutions. In order to bring to book the deeply corrupt officers who were the subject of investigation, some of the A10 officers used bullying tactics on junior officers whom they believed were in possession of knowledge which could be used as evidence against the crooked cops, although, of course, this might not necessarily have been the case.

Naturally, there were decent, hard-working officers at A10 who were determined to achieve success in the fight against corruption without resorting to these types of tactics, but there was an aura of fear enveloping the Metropolitan Police. Officers were being returned to uniform on the flimsiest of evidence and sometimes their careers were ruined on the basis of rumours alone. Incredibly, these despotic actions became a two-way street; if a detective was thought to be behaving not in a dishonest but in a recalcitrant or bolshie manner, he could be threatened with a posting to A10. The threat was usually quite sufficient to make the most contumacious offender toe the line.

In consequence, the whole of A10, good cops as well as bad ones, were lumped together and cordially disliked. No-one trusted them. The good guys out on the streets – and this was the vast majority of the Metropolitan Police's 3,200 detectives – wanted the bad ones turfed out (and the sooner the better) but because of the mistrust that had arisen no one wanted to volunteer information of wrongdoing to A10. No, the unit which was going to 'clear up the Met' had more than a whiff of McCarthyism about it.

Ten years passed and the complaints department was now known as CIB2. The bullying, blustering officers of yesteryear had more or less vanished and the whole department was now known to have adopted a stronger, more professional approach. There was of course no question of corrupt behaviour in the Waldorf case; however, because the whole affair seriously threatened the public's credibility of the police, CIB2 was quite rightly called in at the earliest opportunity.

At 1.25 on the morning of Saturday 15 January, the still-shocked Peter Finch was interviewed by Detective Chief Superintendent Neil Dickens from CIB2. Dickens was then 42 and during his twenty-six years' service with Hertfordshire Constabulary he had been commended on thirteen occasions for his work in catching criminals while serving in uniform, in the CID and also the Regional Crime Squad. Now, in a sideways move to the Metropolitan Police, he would spend a twelve months' attachment with CIB2.

The notes were recorded contemporaneously by Detective Sergeant William Hose and Finch was asked, by Dickens, referring to Martin, 'What type of man is he?'

'I think he is a very dangerous man with no regard to the law or authority,' replied Finch, adding 'and at the time of his arrest he said that he could have taken a number of officers with him. I would say that he would not hesitate to use violence, i.e. firearms, to make good his escape.'

To make the point quite clear, Dickens said, 'Did he make the comments personally to you, or is it something you have heard?'

Finch replied, 'Referring to my pocketbook, he said upon arrest whilst I was struggling with him, he said to me, "I'll have you, I'll blow you away," so I know from first-hand experience that he wouldn't hesitate to shoot a police officer.'

He was asked to detail his duties of the previous day, and he did so, and stated that the reason why he had drawn his gun was because he was wearing a large blue anorak over his holster and that he might well have experienced difficulty – as indeed he would – in drawing his weapon if he was confronted by Martin. 'Why,' he was asked, 'did you consider it necessary to draw your weapon?'

'I knew that if the man was Martin that he might well have a gun in his hand,' replied Finch, adding decisively, 'and he would shoot me first before I had time to draw my weapon.'

Although Finch's actions in Pembroke Road have already been mentioned in the narrative of this book, it is important to see precisely what he had to say to his questioner:

> I had my gun in my right hand, close to my leg. As I approached the Volkswagen van which was in the nearside lane, I saw the yellow Marina van of Central 415 and the passenger shouted to me, 'It's the yellow Mini in front of the van.' They were about two cars behind the van in the same line of traffic. I then slowed down my pace and approached the Mini from the rear nearside. I could see that the driver was a male and there was another male in the front passenger seat. I walked up to the front passenger's door and I looked at him and I was convinced it was Martin. I was slightly behind him. I saw his nose which was rather large. I then backed off to the Mini's rear nearside and as I did so, the driver turned round and looked at me and said something. I got myself into the drawn weapons position and I crouched very low. I did call out 'Armed Police' but could not say anything further because I saw the man who I thought was Martin turn to the rear seat and I thought he was going to reach for a gun and I feared for my life. As he did so, I fired a paired shot and these went into the rear nearside tyre.

'Did you see a gun?' asked Dickens, 'or anything that resembled a gun in the car?'

'No, I did not,' replied Finch. 'It was just his sudden movement which I saw. I then raised myself from a low position and moved towards his passenger window. He was shouting something and still moving, so I fired two paired shots towards his left arm at close range.'

Dickens later asked: 'You described how this man moved and shouted. Did you get the opportunity of a good look at him?'

'Yes, when I was at the passenger window,' replied Finch. 'I saw him in profile, although the street wasn't that well lit and I was still convinced that he was Martin.'

At the end of the seventy-five-minute interview, Finch was cautioned, that is, that he need not say anything more unless he wished to do so and that whatever he said would be taken down in writing and might be given in evidence, and he declined to do so.

The next interview, again conducted by Dickens, was at 9.32 that evening, in the presence of Finch's solicitor, Ian Walker of Russell, Jones & Walker, the solicitors invariably instructed by the Police Federation to act for accused officers. The notes were contemporaneously recorded by Detective Sergeant Gus MacKenzie and this time Finch was cautioned from the outset.

He was led through the police regulations about when it was proper to draw a gun from one's holster and then Finch was asked if, when he went out on foot, it was 'solely for the purpose of making a positive identification?' The question was slightly ambiguous because at the briefing it had been stated that if Martin had become aware of a police presence, he might well have to be arrested on the street, hence five officers being armed. But Finch's answer was equally obscure, because he replied, 'I wouldn't say that it was solely for that purpose because it had been discussed on a number of occasions that if we were on the street, we would take him,' which was not necessarily the case.

'How many other officers were sent out on foot?' asked Dickens.

'As I was the closest unit, other than the surveillance team and the fact that Detective Sergeant Hockaday whom I was with did not know him, when I heard the call it was agreed between us that I would go on foot,' replied Finch. 'I did not hear anyone else say they would be going on foot to give assistance.'

Dickens suggested once again that the object was merely to give Finch the chance of having a look in the car and Finch replied, 'That may have been the object, but when I saw who I thought was Martin, I decided I could cope.'

Referring back to Finch's explanation as to when it was proper to draw a gun from its holster, if it was intended to use it, Dickens asked, 'Had you made such an intention?'

'I had decided that if the need arose, yes, I would use my firearm,' answered Finch.

He told the interviewing officer that he had shouted a warning and because of the passenger's actions he thought he was going for a weapon: he believed that seeing him in the 'drawn weapons' position, would make them stop what they were doing and surrender. 'They had little time to surrender,' commented Dickens but as Finch replied, 'Yes, I agree, but I thought my life was in danger.'

Finch went on to explain that as he went round to the driver's door of the Mini, he could see Waldorf moving, half out of the car; he could see Deane was carrying out a 'reload' and would therefore be incapable of bringing his gun into use again; he (Finch) was out of ammunition and because he felt the man still represented a danger, he struck him several times on the head with his revolver. He then reloaded his weapon and covered the man while he was handcuffed. It was only when he looked at the man full in the face that he realised that man was not David Martin.

Dickens suggested that Finch had lost control of himself at that time, discharging his firearm at an innocent man whose identity he had mistaken and had followed it up by setting about him bodily with his gun, but Finch replied, 'I do not think I had lost control of myself. I knew what I was doing all the time,' and shortly afterwards the interview concluded after forty-nine minutes.

Following Finch's preliminary interview, Jardine was interviewed by Detective Chief Inspector Brian Siddle of CIB2 and Detective Sergeant Thomas Yates contemporaneously recorded the questions and answers, which commenced at 3.22 a.m.

During the questioning, Jardine said that he had seen Finch pass him on foot in Pembroke Road, gun drawn, and then, 'I think I was distracted momentarily, either by the radio or moving the car or something but when I looked at him again, he was pointing his gun at the Mini and shots were being fired.' Jardine told Siddle that he assumed that a positive identification had been made, that the man inside the Mini had a gun and from the number of shots which had been fired, that the passenger was firing back. Describing how Deane had got out of the car and had gone to the Mini's nearside, Jardine stated he had also run towards the Mini, drawing his revolver as he did so. 'DC Finch was to the offside of the Mini and to the offside of the man who was sprawled half in and half out,' he told Siddle.

'What happened then?' he was asked and Jardine replied, 'I assumed the man had been shot but he was still moving. Because of the briefing and because of what I knew of the man, I still considered him to be very dangerous and I fired two shots towards his head. He was still moving after that, so I fired a further shot towards his head. I didn't see if any of these shots hit him, but his movements certainly became a lot slower.'

The interview concluded at 4.10 a.m. but twenty minutes later, Jardine was again interviewed, this time by Detective Chief Superintendent Dickens who had just read the notes of his interview. A few more questions were asked, mainly with regards to what he may have said to the occupants of the car and his reasoning behind shooting Waldorf; he was then cautioned and the interview concluded.

Later the same day, at 6.55 p.m., Dickens interviewed Jardine again and, in keeping with Finch's later interview, Jardine was cautioned from the outset. He was not legally represented but he had the services of a Police Federation representative, Police Constable 501 'TD' Reginald Jenkins, who thirteen years previously while serving as a C11 motorcyclist had been awarded a British Empire Medal for gallantry during a shootout with bank robbers in South London.

It was an exceptionally short interview, because Jardine told Dickens, ' ... as you are aware, I was interviewed until about 5 a.m. this morning, after which I was officially cautioned. I do not wish to obstruct this inquiry in any way but in view of the serious nature of the incident and the fact that I was strongly advised by senior officers to obtain legal advice, which I have not yet had the opportunity to do, I must with great regret decline to answer any further questions until I have legal representation. I would like to add that I have a complete answer for any action I took, which I will give at a later date.'

That 'later date' came three days afterwards when Jardine was again interviewed, this time by Commander Michael Bradley Taylor of CIB2, the officer in charge of the complaints unit. At the time of this investigation, Taylor was 42 years of age, having joined the police in 1960. His rise through the service had been meteoric; initially a detective, his results in the sergeant's examination were so spectacularly high that he returned to uniform and shot up through the ranks. He would not return to the CID until reaching the rank of detective superintendent; since then he had served two terms with the Flying Squad. He was much admired as being a hard-working, practical copper.

For a matter as serious as this, Taylor would normally have immediately taken charge of all the interviews, but when he heard the names of the officers involved in the shooting, he immediately realised that he knew Peter Finch personally from the mid-1960s and therefore he made this fact known and dealt instead with Jardine, hence Dickens's involvement with Finch. Dickens was also present for the Jardine interview, as was a solicitor, Mr Roscoe.

Taylor took him through his service and then the detailed briefing given by Ness which Jardine once more described, ending with the words, 'To my mind, the overall effect of the briefing was to paint a picture of an extremely dangerous and unstable person.'

Again Jardine was taken through following the Mini and he said:

> … I asked DC Deane who the driver was and he told me it was Purdy. I think I asked who the other person was in the front passenger seat and I think DC Deane said something to the effect, 'I don't know, I haven't seen him before' … I seem to recall saying to DC Deane, 'from the hairstyle, that could almost be our main man', meaning Martin. DC Deane and I discussed that and I think DC Deane put it up over the radio as to whether anyone else thought it might be Martin … In the Bayswater Road, on the approach to the Shepherd's Bush roundabout where I was able to get alongside the Mini, from that position we could see the man in profile, although most of the time our view was blocked by the driver of the Mini. However, from the hair, eyes and nose of the man in the Mini, DC Deane and I formed the opinion that this man was a good likeness for the man Martin. At about that point, DC Deane put it over the radio that it was a possibility that the man in the front passenger seat was Martin.

After a coffee break, Jardine said, 'Another point we were told about Martin during the briefing was that on a previous occasion he had been shot by police, on that occasion I understood he was hit in the head by a bullet which deviated to the collar bone and broke it. I was told that on that occasion, Martin seemed to suffer little reaction to the wound, in that he did not go into shock or complain of any pain. I drew the conclusion from that, that when confronted Martin would be a difficult man to stop.'

The questioning continued up to the point when the traffic was stationary in Pembroke Road and that Finch had been detailed to attempt an identification of Martin. 'Were you aware of any instructions from Mr Ness at this point?' asked Taylor and Jardine replied, 'Not personally. No, but it's quite difficult trying to listen to two radios and drive and keep the vehicle in sight, all at the same time.' He could also have added the difficulty of concentrating while the other units on both radios, plus the CB gibberish, was being transmitted, in addition to the responsibility of the loaded revolver in the shoulder holster under his left armpit.

'DC Deane wound down his window and shouted something like, "it's a few cars in front of us, in front of the white van",' continued Jardine. 'By then, DC Finch was level with us and I could see that he had a revolver in his right hand, holding it alongside his right thigh. I was astonished to see that he had drawn his gun and DC Deane and I commented to each other about that.'

After he heard the sound of shots being fired, Jardine said, 'I thought, "God, that's Martin, he's got a gun and he's firing".'

He went on to describe once more getting out of the van and seeing Waldorf hanging out of the driver's door. 'I was convinced that the man had a gun very close to him, probably under his body,' said Jardine, adding, 'he *must* have had a gun, otherwise no shots would have been fired in the first place. Because of his movements, I was convinced that he was going to get hold of a gun and start shooting again. I was desperately afraid that he was going to shoot either me or DC Finch who at that time would have been within Martin's line of fire,' and once more described shooting Waldorf.

'Did you see a gun or any other weapons at any stage, other than police weapons?' asked Taylor and Jardine answered, 'No.'

And then Taylor said: 'When you fired on Waldorf, what did you intend?'

'I intended to totally incapacitate him,' replied Jardine, 'and the only way to do that with a gun is to kill him.'

'So – bluntly,' said Taylor, 'your intention was to kill him, if necessary?'

'If necessary, yes,' he replied.

'Listen to this,' said Taylor, picking up a copy of the police firearms regulations. '"Every officer to whom a weapon is issued must be strictly warned that it is to be used only in cases of absolute necessity, e.g. if he, or the person he is protecting, is attacked by a person with a firearm or other deadly weapon and he cannot otherwise reasonably protect himself or give protection, he may resort to a firearm as a means of defence." Are you aware of that instruction?'

'Yes, sir,' replied Jardine.

'At the time you fired at Waldorf, were you or anybody else being attacked?'

'No, but I had considered that an attack had just taken place,' replied Jardine, 'and I was certain that that attack was about to begin again.'

Asked to account for his following actions, Jardine described covering Stephens in case she had any weapons and was also asked if he thought it necessary for Finch to have pistol-whipped Waldorf. 'I'm not sure whether I considered it necessary for DC Finch to hit Waldorf, but I do remember thinking, "Christ, he's still moving!"'

'At the briefing, was it ever suggested in these or in any other similar terms that if Martin was located, any armed officer should shoot first?' asked Taylor and Jardine emphatically replied, 'Absolutely not.'

'There was no suggestion of that nature at all?' probed Taylor and once more Jardine replied, 'Absolutely not.'

There were more questions and then when Taylor asked, 'Did you ever tell Waldorf that you were a police officer or call on him to surrender before you opened fire?' Jardine replied, 'No, I considered things had gone far beyond that.'

Jardine finished by reiterating that he had acted totally in good faith and Taylor commented on his frankness.

It was inescapable that both Jardine and Finch would be charged because someone had to be seen to be publicly accountable and when it happened, it did so very quickly. Eight minutes after the conclusion of Jardine's interview, Taylor told him that a decision had been made by the Director of Public Prosecutions to charge him with attempted murder and thirty-three minutes after that, he was at Rochester Row police station. Thirteen minutes later, at nine o'clock, Finch was charged with attempting to wound Steven Waldorf and the men both appeared at Horseferry Road Magistrates' Court the following day.

John Deane (who had qualified as a marksman in 1973) had been similarly interviewed by Detective Superintendent Douglas Pike of CIB2, and following that interview a further one took place on Saturday 15 January by Detective Chief Superintendent Dickens in which Deane was immediately cautioned. The questioning led right up to when the shooting began.

'[T]he next thing that happened was that a shot rang out,' said Deane. 'I then got out of the van as quickly as possible and on the pavement I then drew my gun, more shots were ringing out and I saw DC Finch firing into the nearside window. I was then quite convinced that the male passenger was Martin and that owing to our briefing about the danger and equipment that this man carried and also to the amount of shooting that seemed to be going on, I went to the rescue of DC Finch. I got to the rear of the Mini and could clearly see the rear of the man I believed to be Martin. There was a lot of movement and I shot two pairs and one single as quickly as possible.'

'Did you see anything in that suspect's possession that resembled a firearm?' asked Dickens and Deane replied, 'No, sir.'

'Therefore,' said Dickens, 'you were discharging your weapon at the back of a person, purely because a fellow officer was shooting at him.'

'No, sir,' firmly repeated Deane. 'I believed that what was going on was that a positive identification had been made and believed that from what I had been told at the original briefing that he was carrying firearms and was using them against DC Finch.'

'Are you trained to use firearms in this way?' asked Dickens and Deane replied, just as decisively as before, 'When I believe that someone is in danger of being killed by another with a weapon or other item, then I acted as I believe I had been trained.'

'Did you give consideration to the safety to other persons in the car?' asked Dickens.

'Susie was lying down on the floor, there was no sign of any other person than the man I believed to be Martin in the vehicle,' replied Deane. 'I had a clear view, unobstructed of this man.'

Deane was suspended from duty, together with the other officers. When the facts were reported to the Director of Public Prosecutions, he decided to take no further action in Deane's case.

However, many police officers – and to be fair, most of them were not in possession of the full facts – thought that the matter had been disposed of with an almost indecent haste. But in speaking to Michael Taylor three decades later, he put the matter in its right context:

> The speed with which the inquiry moved was due to the interview statements being typed up and the initial report put together quickly; I wrote it at home once the interviews were complete and submitted it, as you say, within a few days. The interviews were conducted briefly on the night of the shooting and then in more depth once the officers had had an opportunity for some sleep and the chance to decide on any representation. The facts were not really in dispute. I was not under any political pressure but reported regularly to the deputy commissioner.[1]

Jardine would later tell me that he thought his interviews were dealt with 'very fairly' whereas Finch told me, 'What I find unbelievable now was how I was treated at the nick. I was interviewed into the early hours with no help whatsoever. Naïvely, I thought I was giving a statement to help before any inquiry.'

Whatever the rights or wrongs of the circumstances surrounding those initial interviews, what I do know is that if an ordinary criminal had been dealt with in exactly the same situation without being cautioned or legally represented, their legal representatives would have had a field day in court. Be that as it may, the interviews had also been thorough and no stone had been left unturned to establish the truth.

---

1. The deputy commissioner was the officer in charge of all aspects of discipline within the Metropolitan Police.

Explanations and Recriminations

I f the charging of the two officers was quick, Scotland Yard's immediate and unequivocal apology for the shooting, issued the same night as the incident, saying it was 'a tragic case of mistaken identity' was positively mercurial, and rightly so.

On Sunday 16 January, a far fuller statement was made by the Yard:

The Metropolitan Police deeply regret that anyone should have been injured as a result of police activities. Police were seeking to arrest David Ralph Martin who had escaped from police custody after being charged with attempted murder by shooting a policeman, armed robbery and burglary involving the theft of handguns and ammunition.

It was known that there was an association between Martin and a passenger in the car which police followed. Having regard to the background, the officers were armed and when the car stopped in heavy traffic, an officer sought to identify Martin and shots were fired. As the precise circumstances of the incident will be the basis of any judgement of criminal or disciplinary liability, they cannot be commented on at this stage. It is already clear, however, that there has been a tragic case of mistaken identity.

Within an hour of the occurrence, Commander Michael Taylor,

head of the Complaints Investigation Branch, commenced an investigation of the case which has since been pursued expeditiously and thoroughly.

Thirty private witnesses have been traced and the majority interviewed. In all some seventy interviews have been completed and on Saturday night the inquiry reached the point where three detectives were suspended.

The results of the investigation will be reported to the independent Director of Public Prosecutions and the lay commissioners of the Independent Police Complaints Board. In addition, a preliminary report has been forwarded to the Home Secretary.

On the general rules of governing the issue and use of firearms it should be said that the procedure is strict. The instructions provide that an inquiry is conducted by a senior officer every time police fire a round of ammunition, and the circumstances are strictly reviewed. Any officer in breach of the rigorous requirements, however technical, is disqualified from the further use of firearms.

There is no cover-up of any incident involving firearms and police share public concern that their use should be wholly exceptional. Police are as anxious as the public that the whole circumstances of this tragic accident should be clarified and as the commissioner has already made plain, the results will be made public when the constraints of the law are lifted.

In answer to some particular allegations, it must be stressed that the current policy on police use of firearms has been in force for some years and there have been no recent changes.

The following day, Detective Constable Gordon Harrison was on reserve in the Flying Squad office where one of the 'For police eyes only' Martin wanted posters was pasted on the wall. The deeply detested Deputy Assistant Commissioner David Powis OBE, QPM – one of Sir Robert Mark's myrmidons – entered the office, removed the poster and took it away, roaring in his usual bellicose manner, 'Too inflammatory!'

And of course the day following the shooting, the newspaper headlines were full of the incident. *The Guardian* rather predictably stated, 'The idea that police shoot first and ask questions later should be entirely foreign to our way of life.' 'Police shoot wrong man in rush hour' were the *Daily Mail*'s headlines. Stephens's flatmate Sue Sykes was quoted as angrily saying, 'Even if it was Dave in the car, the police shouldn't just shoot him like that.' *The Sunday Times* told their readers that the shooting was 'a disaster waiting to happen'. Mrs Marilyn Brown was taking her baby into St Stephen's Hospital when she saw Stephens brought in in handcuffs and heard her say, 'I don't know why they had to shoot him.' That, said the *Daily Mail*, was the question to which everyone wanted an answer.

The Monday edition of that newspaper attempted to provide those answers when in an exclusive interview Sue Stephens's version of her relationship with Martin and her account of the shooting were published; 'Who have we shot?' were the headlines: 'Girl in the Mini tells first full story: "Police were exultant, then it was all just horror and fright"' and it continued into the Tuesday edition. Much of that edition was given to Stephens's peripatetic lifestyle plus details of the film stars, singers and other glitterati she had encountered along the way. She was keen to stress that Martin was not a transvestite; photos of him dressed as a woman, she said, 'were taken at a fancy dress drag party'. Stephens had also informed the *Daily Mail*'s readers that Martin had made his escape from the cell at Great Marlborough Street court by using a key which he had made himself. 'He's been in the cell before and seen the jailer using the key,' she said. 'He's only got to see something once and he can copy it from memory. He's incredible. He can open handcuffs with his fingernails. It's a game he plays with the authorities.'

Not only was this nationwide news, it was covered worldwide, with an account of the shooting in the US State of Maine's newspaper the *Lewiston Daily Sun*, and also Pennsylvania's *Observer-Reporter* who informed their readers that 'On Friday, police leapt from a truck and opened fire on the car Waldorf had just rented' and furthermore, 'The shootout has raised allegations from opposition legislators that the police were evidently "determined to kill" Martin.'

Monday's headlines of the *Daily Express* were conciliatory: 'This Tragic Mistake'; 'The police and Steven Waldorf – a case of mistaken identity' and carried photographs of both Waldorf and Martin. However, the opinion page contained in the Scottish edition of the newspaper said, in part: 'The policemen involved in the Kensington shoot-out ought to be severely punished. They deserve no less for what they apparently did was unforgivable …' and Waldorf's parents agreed. 'We can't forgive the police for this,' they said. 'It may be a mistake to them, but it is a tragedy for us.'

The *Daily Mirror* was far more accusing. 'WHY,' it thundered, 'didn't police try bloodless arrest moments earlier?' Lester Purdy provided what could have been the answer to this rhetorical question: 'Steven had waited on the pavement for ten minutes while I was inside the building, arranging to hire the car.'

'HOW,' further demanded the *Mirror*, 'could they mistake the two men?' Film director Tony Parker, a former colleague of Steven Waldorf's, dismissively supplied his opinion to that conundrum: 'It would be like mistaking Ronnie Corbett for Ronnie Barker,' although as one police officer sourly commented, 'Waldorf looked more like Martin than Martin.' This sentiment was echoed by Robert Darby who coincidentally several years later, while on holiday in the Mediterranean, saw Waldorf, who was talking about the incident and showed the listeners the scars from his bullet wounds. Darby had not seen Waldorf before, whereas Martin he had seen on several occasions. 'If I had been Finch when he went up to that Mini,' he told me, 'I would have taken exactly the same action as he did. Waldorf and Martin were *doppelgängers*.'

Two separate enquiries were ordered; and in the House, the Shadow Home Secretary Roy Hattersley PC, MP, FRSL (later Baron Hattersley) asked the Home Secretary, William Whitelaw KT, CH, MC, PC, DL (later 1st Viscount Whitelaw):

> To understand that the nationwide concern that has been expressed about last Friday's tragedy involves not only the shooting of one innocent man but the practices and procedures that made that tragedy possible? I therefore ask the Home Secretary to understand that the House, like the country, expects an inquiry into the regulations governing the use of firearms to police officers and … that he must tell us how he … proposes to remedy the problems that allowed it to happen in the first place?

The Home Secretary announced that a full report would be sent to the Police Complaints Department and the Director of Public Prosecutions, Sir Thomas Hetherington KCB, CBE, QC, TD, telling the members, 'All steps will be taken to ensure no such incident should ever happen again.' A bristling Paul Boateng PC, MP (later Lord Boateng), never the most enthusiastic supporter of the police despite being a member of the Greater London Council's Police Committee, stated that the incident raised serious questions regarding police orders governing firearms. The Commissioner, Sir Kenneth Leslie Newman GBE, QPM, KStJ, LLB, CIMGT, who had just taken up the post a few months previously, mentioned that there might be a close review of police gun controls; he was right.

All these accusations and condemnations were aired on Monday 17 January and there would be far more to come. There was immense public sympathy for Steven Waldorf – again, rightly so. However, within rank-and-file police circles there was enormous concern for the two officers, where the old maxim 'There, but for the grace of God, go I' was freely utilised. American police officers have an even more prescient saying: 'Better to be judged by twelve, than carried by six.'

The officers had had to make a split-second decision – something their pompous, postulating critics never have to do – and in that blinking of an eye, with no time to issue a regulation police warning, had made a terrible and catastrophic mistake.

'What bad luck for Peter,' Bob Cook told me thirty years later. 'He was a fine, brave cop who loved his work and, because of David Martin, his life was damaged completely.' Also referring to Peter Finch, Steve Fletcher said to me, 'He struck me as being an undemonstrative, conscientious detective. A good copper.'

John Devine agreed. 'I felt really sorry for him,' he remarked. 'He was a lovely individual and a true gentleman,' and with regards to Finch going forward on foot to try to identify Martin in Pembroke Road, he opined, 'which in my view was a big mistake,' feeling that 'he was placed in an invidious position'.

'I knew John Jardine from 'X' Division,' Colin Hockaday told me. 'I also knew him from combined operations between the Flying Squad and C11. My opinion of him was that he was very level-headed, was good at what he did, with a good sense of humour; there wasn't an ounce of malice in him.'

Matters had reached a state of almost militant resentment when a meeting was held at Elliot House, a police section house for unmarried officers. Feeling that Finch had been shabbily treated, the mood among the assembled officers was that firearms officers should hand in their authorisations. An officer of commander rank arrived, apprehensively asked if members of the press were present and having established there were not, gave the assembled officers a pep talk, to the effect that if they were to do so, it would be putting their colleagues at risk from the growing culture of gun crime. Growling mutinously, the officers dispersed without any authorisations being surrendered; but as the Iron Duke might have mentioned on that occasion, as he did at Waterloo, 'It has been a damned nice thing – the nearest run thing you ever saw in your life …'

Anthony Blok, Martin's solicitor, appealed to his client to contact him, in order that he could arrange 'safe custody' for him. 'He has just cause to be afraid for his life,' said Mr Blok, but if Martin heard this impassioned plea, he ignored it.

He might have been in the seaside town of Paignton, Devon; that was where an off-duty detective believed that he saw him on Tuesday 18 January. The alarm was raised but as darkness fell, by the end of a six-hour operation, which included armed police officers, the operation was stood down. A spokesman for the Devon and Cornwall Constabulary stated, 'There is a possibility that Martin could be in the area and we are still keeping an eye open for him; after all, his girlfriend came from close by.'

By 19 January, Waldorf had been able to breathe for about an hour a day without the support of a ventilator. A hospital spokesman stated: 'Although still in a serious condition, he has had a comfortable and stable day and his progress has been maintained.'

The second of the inquiries was to appoint the Flying Squad to lead the hunt for David Martin.

Enter the Flying Squad

The Flying Squad had been formed in 1919 as a new mobile unit to combat the sudden upsurge in crime following the end of the First World War. For the first time, detectives were able to travel rapidly from one hotspot of crime in London to another. Within ten years, they had become a household name. Whatever they did became headline news and with their fast cars – Bentleys, Lagondas and Invictas – their use of informants and knowledge of the underworld, they quickly became established as the Metropolitan Police's premier crime-busting department. Tough and uncompromising, and said by their critics to be unorthodox, they took on the toughest gangs and won.

These included the raid at London's newly opened Heathrow Airport in 1948 – it became known as 'The Battle of Heathrow' – when an attempt was made to steal gold bullion and other commodities valued at £487,900. It resulted in commendations for the Sweeney and a total of seventy-one years' penal servitude for the eight-strong gang. The squad struck again fifteen years later; the seventeen persons convicted for their parts in the massive £2,631,684 Great Train Robbery were awarded a total of a staggering 369 years' imprisonment.

The use of informants was put to the test when the highly secretive post-war Ghost Squad was formed in 1946 by four members of the Flying Squad. In less than four years, the rings of black marketeers, lorry hijackers and warehousebreakers were smashed, with 727 arrests carried out and property valued by today's standards at £10 million being recovered.

The squad were particularly adroit at arresting escapees from custody; in 1940, Charles 'Ruby' Sparks was arrested after a record-breaking absence of six months from Dartmoor prison and when master safe-breaker Alfie Hinds escaped from Nottingham prison while serving twelve years' preventative detention, the Flying Squad brought him back. Train robber Charlie Wilson made a spectacular escape from Winson Green prison; once again it was the Sweeney who traced him to Canada and arrested him.

The Squad had always been in the public eye; when the television series *The Sweeney*, starring John Thaw and Dennis Waterman, was first shown in 1975, it was so popular that it ran for four series and spawned two films. And when the Channel Four programme *Flying Squad*, in which a camera crew accompanied Flying Squad officers on operations, was broadcast in 1989, it attracted an audience of 12 million viewers.

If anyone was going to bring David Martin to book, it was going to be the Flying Squad.

Nowadays, when I look back at those halcyon days of the Flying Squad at the Yard – the happiest days of my police service – I suppose I could be accused of viewing them through rose-tinted spectacles. It's an understandable accusation, but like many other indictments levelled against me, it's untrue. Because when I recall my Squad contemporaries, the vast majority were the finest comrades a detective could ask for. Tough, shrewd, brave and knowledgeable in the ways of the underworld, they were relentless in their pursuit of criminals and contemptuous of them and their lawyers, of whom only a law degree often separated them from their clients.

Never once, when we bashed in doors, never fully sure of what we were going to find on the other side, was I apprehensive. Never once, when the superlative Class I trained drivers drove us across London at gasp-producing speeds, did I flinch. I was in the company of men, rascals some of them, but who would never let me down and whom I could, and often did, trust with my life.

Men like Detective Sergeant John Redgrave, a six foot five colossus who had boxed for the Lafone Cup, whom I described as being 'as tough as woodpecker's lips'; he and Detective Sergeant Alan Branch and Detective Constable Mick Geraghty had recently been commended by the commissioner for bravery and devotion to duty, for arresting and disarming, while unarmed themselves, two highly dangerous armed robbers. These and many more like them were the calibre of the officers I had working with me. David Martin's days of freedom were numbered.

The commander of the squad, Frank Cater, was 53 years of age. The former Royal Marine had thirty years' service with the Metropolitan Police at the time of the shooting and was a career detective, having been part of the teams who had brought about the downfall of the Richardson gang and the Kray brothers. ('I soon realised his great potential,' said 'Nipper' Read, 'and made him my Number Two.') This was Cater's first posting to the Flying Squad; a committed fraud investigator, he had a calm, methodical approach to enquiries. So when he said to me, 'We need to wind this up as soon as possible, Dick,' it was out of the ordinary for him. A few days later he was interviewed by the *Daily Express* and he said, 'How dangerous is he? Well, he stands charged with shooting a police officer. As to whether he would shoot at a member of the public … I wouldn't know,' it was the normal, laid-back Frank Cater type of reply.

Perhaps that remark was used to try to dampen down the flames being generated by the media. First, there was cross-dressing, bisexual David Martin, a serial escaper, a chameleon of disguise who had already shot a police officer. Next, there was his girlfriend, a glamorous former model and dancer who had told the press that her life had been saved in the Mini because she had been wearing a leather and metal juju charm, following a chance meeting with an African witchdoctor. There was the public concern regarding an innocent man who had been shot by police, two of whom had been charged with his attempted murder. It was a headline story that would run and run until Martin was caught.

Detective Constable Mick Geraghty was part of a Flying Squad surveillance team and at the time of being called to Paddington Green, he and Police Constable Chris Colbourne (a former 10 Squad driver) had been working to discover the whereabouts of two suspects in the Deptford area who had shot at police officers – now that inquiry had to be left to others on the team. Geraghty and Colbourne's job was to set up an OP to cover Enter's address at St Charles' Square, Ladbroke Grove and for that they used the tower of the local fire station. The OP was manned from 6 a.m. until midnight by the officers; in addition, they had technical help in the form of a time-lapse camera. Every morning, they reviewed the tape for the time not visually covered by them and informed the incident room of their findings; in turn, they were kept up to date with the progress of the inquiry.

Geraghty and Colbourne maintained watch on the premises for six or seven days; it was, said Geraghty, 'A tiring, uncomfortable and freezing OP. The small window we watched out of was broken and when the wind blew, our eyes would water a lot.'

On Saturday 22 January, the officers came on duty and as usual checked the tape. It revealed that a man matching Martin's description had entered the address at one o'clock that morning. Don Brown and some other senior officers arrived at the OP to check the tape themselves; it appeared it was a possibility that Martin was in the building and the firearms unit D11 was called, as were available Flying Squad units.

I was in a Flying Squad car when we received the call and as Steve Holloway recalled, 'We were at Barking and got the call to go there and Tony Freeman got us there in about twenty minutes.'

It was necessary to know if there was any other access to the flat other than the front door and Geraghty was tasked to find this out. 'I did this by approaching a lady after she left the building from the ground floor,' Geraghty told me. 'She walked around the corner to her car and I introduced myself as a police officer. She looked at me in horror. I looked knackered, dirty, unshaven, wearing old camouflage clothes, but after producing my warrant card and hearing my story, she agreed to let me into the flats.'

Geraghty was invited up to the woman's flat and was able to keep the basement under observation. He used his covert body set to keep the rest of us apprised of the situation while matters developed and when they did, they developed very quickly. My team, together with other Flying Squad officers, had arrived, Geraghty opened the ground-floor front door to permit access to a D11 officer to cover any escape through the building and then an armoured D11 Land Rover pulled up outside the premises. The street had been sealed off and local residents were told to stay indoors. A telephone call was put into the flat to inform them of the presence of armed police officers and for them to come out immediately, separately with their hands up, then kneel and then lie down. We then stepped in and dealt with them. Martin was not one of the three, nor was he in the building. What was in the building was some of the property stolen by Martin, deposited there just over two weeks previously. Two of the three occupants of the flat – a man and a woman – were released. The third, whose name was Peter Enter, was not.

It was not too long before Susie Stephens was arrested. She went to Paddington Green police station by appointment on 23 January and as soon as she arrived, was cautioned and charged. And on the evening of 24 January as Lester Purdy finished visiting Steven Waldorf at St Stephen's Hospital, he heard his name called from a parked car. He walked over, looked inside and made the acquaintance of Steve Holloway who without further ado, pulled him inside, informing him that he too was under arrest.

My team were armed on a permanent basis. I've mentioned Detective Constable Steve Holloway, a tough, Hoxton-born East Ender with a thick, black moustache whose complexion was so swarthy that I often suggested that Greek blood was present in his genetic make-up; coincidentally, he spoke Greek quite well. Detective Sergeant John Redgrave too has already been mentioned; he would go on to receive immense kudos when effecting the arrest of an armed robber from East London with a terrifying reputation for mindless violence; Redgrave simply picked him up and threw him against a door. However, since the door was made of plate glass, the concussion of the robber's body against it caused the door to be shattered. Amazingly, he recovered in time to stand trial.

We, together with our driver Tony Freeman, were on standby at Paddington Green police station to act on any tip-offs as to Martin's whereabouts from members of the public. With us were

Detective Sergeant Alan Branch, another very tough customer, and Detective Constable Gerry Gallagher. Gerry was a wonderful asset to any dangerous situation due in no small part to his voice – like the Greek god Pan, whose angry shout when disturbed an afternoon nap was enough to inspire 'panic'. He and I had bashed in the front door of a North London dwelling, frequented by an armed robber. In the hallway, the house's occupier advanced towards us, knife in hand. Gerry, who had drawn his revolver, would I suppose have been quite within his rights to have shot him; however, there was no need. Gerry simply shouted at him and his voice was so thunderous, the knifeman was frozen to the spot and dropped his weapon. I couldn't help but think that with a few more men like Gerry, there would be no need for the issue of pepper sprays and tasers and we'd have many fewer firearm incidents. Alan (referred to variously as 'Branchy' or 'Twiggy') and Gerry were in Central 952, driven by Police Constable John 'Dickie' Dawson who had been awarded a BEM for gallantry after disarming a gunman who had shot at him.

Because of the amount of publicity generated by the case, there were quite a few calls into the inquiry office. A woman telephoned saying she had just seen a man dressed as a woman in Pembroke Road, close to the scene of the shooting; but if she had, there was no sign of him (or her) by the time we arrived. One telephone call came from the manager of a hotel. 'A bloke's just checked in to my hotel,' he said apprehensively, 'but he's dressed as a woman – do you think it could be David Martin?' We decided to find out, and a very surprised transvestite had a model 36 Smith & Wesson shoved up his left nostril. 'Gracious!' he gasped. 'What a fright you gave me!' Much the same scenario was enacted when a combined weight of about forty stone of Flying Squad leant heavily on another hotel room door and the occupant, a bewigged cross-dresser, found himself dragged down to the ground. 'O-o-o-h!' he cried adding,

'I do hope that's a gun you've just shoved in my ear!' Once we established he wasn't Martin, we helped him to his feet, dusted him down and apologised. However, we did have to shell out for a new set of black fishnet stockings because the originals had been irreparably damaged on the way down to the carpet.

On 27 January we got a very firm lead; Martin had attempted to procure a false passport from the Passport Office at Petty France, just around the corner from the Yard, using the tried and tested formula depicted in Frederick Forsyth's 1971 thriller *The Day of the Jackal* – using the identity of a dead person with a year of birth near to Martin's own. This birth certificate had been presented with an application form, together with alleged verification in the form of a North London vicar's signature. It might have worked – but it didn't. An official became suspicious and telephoned police.

A large-scale operation was set up to nab Martin when he returned for the passport: five OPs containing twelve officers, eleven squad vehicles containing twenty-seven officers (nine of them armed) plus fifteen additional C11 personnel. At that time, eight 42s (covert motorcycles) used by C11 were the total number for the whole of the Metropolitan Police District; six of them were deployed in this operation.

It was all to no avail; if Martin did arrive, his finely tuned sixth sense probably advised him to vanish down St James' Park Underground station, which did not have an OP, a car or a surveillance officer on foot covering the entrances. The significance of this oversight becomes apparent in the next chapter.

What appeared to be just as promising was the telephone call I received from the manager of a very upmarket hotel. 'I hope I'm not wasting your time,' he said, 'but a couple have booked into the hotel and they've given their names as Mr and Mrs David Martin.'

'What do they look like?' I asked.

'Oh, he's about thirty, I suppose, about five nine, slim, with blond hair,' he replied, adding, 'and she's a pretty blond.'

'Are they in their room, now?' I said and the manager replied, 'Yes, but I believe they may be going out.'

I put the phone down, thinking furiously. Over the past few days, I'd been finding out quite a bit about Martin. Coolness in a tricky situation – well, I knew all about that from my previous encounter with him and he'd demonstrated it in spades at the time of the PC Carr shooting. Arrogance? Yes. A massive ego? Too right. It would not be beyond the bounds of possibility for Martin to book into a classy hotel like this one, giving his real name and if nothing happened, to telephone the press the following day, telling them that he'd put himself on a plate for the police and *still* they'd been unable to catch him.

But if something *did* happen – what then? Was Martin trying to lure us into a situation where he could have a shootout? It was possible, and there were still those five missing handguns, plus an awful lot of ammunition. The manager thought the couple might soon be going out, so no time to organise a D11 team. All these thoughts had gone through my mind in a matter of seconds with no time for prevarication.

'Gerry! Branchy!' I called out to Gerry Gallagher and Alan Branch. 'Grab some shooters and a driver – come on!' We got into our cars and we roared out of Paddington Green and into the heart of Mayfair.

'Are they still in their room?' I asked the manager and he nodded, sweat beading his upper lip as he looked at the half-dozen scowling desperadoes forming a semi-circle around him in the hotel foyer. Some passing guests also gave us apprehensive glances before slotting us into the 'bad news' category and hurrying away.

'Perhaps … perhaps, I should telephone them and ask them to …' he started to suggest before Steve Holloway fixed him with a baleful look. 'You go anywhere near a phone, mate,' he growled, 'and I'll …' and I gave him a look and shook my head. A good man in a tricky situation, Holloway could be a little impulsive with his comments.

'Just take us up to the room,' I told the manager and up we went, leaving a couple of authorised shots downstairs in case Martin was coming down as we were going up.

We were shown the outside of the room; at my request, the manager opened up a nearby unoccupied, similar room so that we could get some idea of the geography. Next, I discovered that the rooms either side of Mr and Mrs Martin's room were occupied; and since bullets can very easily go through walls, I asked the manager quietly and without any fuss to get the guests out of the rooms. This he did, and as the bemused guests left their rooms their eyes bulged in astonishment at the very determined-looking men dressed in the type of clothing which failed to conform to the hotel's dress code.

The corridor was clear and the shots downstairs were called up and took their place outside the door. Gerry Gallagher, revolver drawn, could hear from an adjoining room the introductory music to the television programme *This is Your Life*. In the event that Martin emerged from the room, brandishing one or more firearms, the thought in his mind, as he later told me, was, 'This *was* your life, mate!'

I went into a vacant room, picked up the telephone and dialled Mr and Mrs Martin's room number.

'David Martin, this is the Flying Squad,' I said, in a voice the *Daily Mail* later described as 'chilling'. 'Your room is surrounded. Get on your hands and knees and open the door. Now!'

David Martin, a slim, blond, 28-year-old singer with the group Hollywood, had just emerged from the bathroom to answer the telephone and was clad only with a towel around his waist. He dutifully got on his hands and knees and started shuffling across the room towards the door. At that moment, his blonde girlfriend, similarly in a state of *semi-déshabillé*, walked out of the bathroom to see her boyfriend performing some very odd antics as he crossed the carpet, endeavouring to struggle into a pair of underpants. Before the thought could cross her mind that this might be some sort of an erotic game in which she could be invited to participate, the door flew open and she saw some of the most frightening looking men in the entire universe, pointing revolvers right at the middle of her paramour's forehead. Realisation immediately set in. 'It's not him!' she screamed and the gun-toting ruffians, after a close inspection of Mr Martin's naked shoulder which revealed no recent gunshot wounds, conceded that he was not.

Soothed with a number of large scotches, supplied by the management, the wholly innocent Mr Martin later told reporters, 'It was terrifying; my life flashed before my eyes. They were so tough and professional. There was no way I was going to try anything on.' Perhaps thinking we might return, he added, 'They were only doing their job and they behaved perfectly.' As an afterthought, he said, 'I might change my name if this goes on much longer!'

This episode prompted a quote from the real David Martin's doting father: 'He escaped for only one thing – his freedom. And now he's got it, he's got to keep on moving. If they want to catch him, they are going to have to do it without my help.'

He also told the *Daily Express*: 'The police have shot one innocent man already. My son is innocent, too – until proven guilty. Since David escaped, he has been branded as viscous – it isn't true.' Cynical, hard-bitten detectives had a hard time swallowing *that* one as no doubt did the shot security guard Edward Burns, Police Constable Carr and Detective Constable Finch.

Later that evening, we were back in action again; a tip-off led us to a Kilburn address at Belsize Road, which, wearing body armour, we duly stormed. 'One minute, everything was quiet,' said resident Michael Claney, 'and the next, the street was being blocked off and police marksmen were diving into doorways.'

But although a man was brought from the house, made to lie down and was frisked, it wasn't Martin; no more than he was at a house in Swiss Cottage which we later surrounded. Late that evening, I sat down in the canteen at Paddington Green police station with a cup of coffee. None of us could relax with a drink; since we could be called out for an armed operation at any moment, at any time of day or night, the thought of alcohol was out of the question. We were getting lots of action but absolutely no results. As I sipped my coffee and stared out at the black, impenetrable night sky over Paddington, I thought, 'You bastard – where are you?'

I thought back to my own successes catching criminals who were on the run. I had always put myself in their position. Where would I go? Who could I go to for help? Where would I hide? Using this logic, I had often succeeded in tracking them down. Martin though was different. He was inventive, he was clever. He had been planning to get a false passport but that had been thwarted. Might he try it again? I shook my head – unlikely. Would he go somewhere else, somewhere outside London? This went round and round in my head; until I thought 'No.' He's here in Paddington, Hampstead, Notting Hill, Belsize Park. I nodded. This is his territory, his habitat. This is where he'll stay, I thought, to take us all on until a final confrontation.

We were unaware of course that our adversary was in a hovel, just over a mile away from us. I've often wondered if at that time

Martin, like a fox gone to earth, was similarly gazing out of the window of that reeking tip of a flat thinking, 'Where can I go? Who will help me? Where can I hide next?' It's possible, but also more than probable that seething with hatred for those hunting him, he was thinking, 'Fuck the lot of you!' Who knows?

'The boys are waiting to go, Sargie.' This was Tony Freeman, who looked at me somewhat askance, probably due to me staring out of the window, muttering and nodding and shaking my head. 'You coming?' I stood up. 'Yes,' I answered. And then, still looking out of the window, I thought once more about Martin's whereabouts. Now I was certain. 'Yes,' I said once more, loudly and I expect Tony thought that I was repeating myself, because he said impatiently, 'Come on, Dick – it's gone midnight.'

I looked at my watch; he was right. It was now Friday, 28 January 1983.

The two faces of David Martin.

Steven Waldorf.

West Hampstead police station, from where Martin re-stole the BMW.

GERALD ROAD (circa 1980)
5 Gerald Road, SW1
Opened 1885
Re-constructed 1925
Closed 1993

Gerald Road police station, from where Martin escaped.

The cell passageway at Marlborough Street Magistrates' Court.

Marlborough Street Magistrates' Court, from where Martin escaped.

Above left: Susan
Stephens.

Above: Commander Frank Cater.

Detective Superintendent
George Ness.

Detective Chief Superintendent Don Brown.

Police Constable Nick Carr.

The author receiving his
fortieth commendation
from Deputy Assistant
Commissioner Michael
Taylor QPM – both
looking strained from
having attended
Detective Inspector
Cam Burnell's funeral.

Detective Constable
John Jardine.

Detective Sergeant Nick Benwell in foreground.

Detective Chief Superintendent Don Brown next to a small boy.

Detective Constable Davy Walker on Martin's right, Detective Constable Steve Holloway with black moustache and Detective Chief Superintendent Don Brown.

Police Constable Tom Renshaw driving Martin away.

Plotting Up

That morning, we took our time getting over to Paddington Green. There had been no urgent phone calls during the night, no 'get here quick, on the double' messages, so we'd all managed to have breakfast with our families and now, showered, shaved and relaxed we arrived at the office mid-morning. There was a lot of laughter and good natured leg-pulling going on; someone had opened that day's edition of *Police Orders* to discover that Gerry Gallagher, Mick Geraghty and Tony Yeoman had been awarded commissioner's commendations for 'bravery and persistence in a case of armed robbery' where the participants had each been sentenced to fourteen years' imprisonment. The chaffing was all a front; those of us in the know were aware that the commendation was very well merited. I'd been an aid to CID with Detective Sergeant Tony Yeoman, who would later achieve immortality after being covertly filmed arresting two armed robbers by the simple expedient of scooping both of them up in his arms and running them into a shop's plate-glass window.

We sat around, checked any possible sightings of Martin and chatted over coffee. Some of the team checked and cleaned their revolvers; but just because I've painted a picture of enforced idleness, it does not mean that nothing was going on in the hunt for Martin. Every piece of information coming in to the investigation was passed to the office manager; no matter how vague or even absurd the intelligence was, it would be entered into an action book and the inquiry allocated to an officer. One such action was a sighting, just a glimpse, of Martin in a brown Ford Sierra; that was all. No registration number, nothing. So it was allocated to 10 Squad's Detective Sergeant Cam Burnell with the directive 'trace the Sierra'.

I liked Cam. At six foot three and weighing sixteen stone, he was a formidable adversary on both the rugby field and in the nabbing of armed robbers. This was demonstrated when we had tackled a gang who were just about to rob a rent collector in East London. The gangleader saw me sprinting towards him and since he knew me well from a previous encounter, he took off like a greyhound. The adrenaline which had flooded into his system had accelerated his flight and I realised he was drawing further and further away from me when suddenly – *Whoosh!* – I was overtaken by Cam. The robber darted round a corner, followed by Cam and when I too rounded the corner, there was the robber lying face down and motionless in the road, with Cam standing over him, his police revolver pointing straight at him and an ominous pall of smoke enveloping them both. Initially, I thought that Cam had shot him but what I was unable to understand was why, being so close behind them, I hadn't heard the sound of the shots. All was soon revealed; first, it was a cold November day and second, the robber had been so traumatised when sixteen-stone Cam landed on his back that he had emptied his bladder – fortunately, it was steam rather than gunsmoke enveloping them. When Cam wasn't battering adversaries on the rugby field or hauling urine-soaked robbers to their feet, he was the best of companions – and what's more, a pretty shrewd detective.

'Trace the Sierra' – an almost impossible task. This is how Cam did it. Martin was driving a brown Sierra. Did it belong to him? Almost certainly not; it had been a long, long time since Martin had surrendered hard cash for a commodity which he could so easily steal. Did it belong to one of his known associates? Their vehicles were checked – no brown Sierra. In any case, who in their right mind, with all the up-to-the-moment publicity would lend their car to Martin? They would believe themselves to be under constant observation by the police, even if this was not the case. Therefore it would be reasonable to assume that the car was stolen. Cam's next step was to sit down with an obliging operator with access to the Police National Computer (PNC).

In the time between Martin's escape from court on 24 December 1982 and the sighting of the car, how many Ford Sierras had been stolen in the United Kingdom? Even though the Sierra range had only been launched three months previously on 15 October 1982, after the PNC operator had rattled her fingers on the keyboard, back came the answer – an awful lot! This was going to take forever, so Cam narrowed down the search. How many had been stolen in the Metropolitan Police District during that time? The answer slimmed down the field, by quite a bit. Next, how many of those Sierras were brown? More were knocked off the list. Next, how many had been recovered prior to the sighting of Martin? The number of stolen brown Sierras was getting less and less. Details of these remaining vehicles were printed off. Cam went through them, one by one, looking for a clue, any hint of a clue. And then, one caught his eye. It had been stolen, just prior to the sighting of Martin, from a car park at Heathrow – exactly from where he had stolen other cars in the past. Bingo. Registration number BYG 780Y. Cam felt this *must* be the one. Of course, Martin could have changed the registration plates – he had done so in the past, as a matter of course – but he would have to have purchased them from a shop and it seemed the whole nation was on full Martin alert. Would he risk doing that? Probably not. So if this was the car that Martin had stolen, Cam had to assume that the original registration plates would still be affixed to it. It was a case full of ifs, ands and buts – it was all Cam had. Details of this vehicle were entered on the PNC with the caveat that if it was seen by police, under no circumstances were they to attempt to stop it or arrest the occupant, but to inform 'Central 899', the Flying Squad switchboard, which in those days was manned twenty-four hours per day, seven days a week.

It was an excellent piece of detective work; and Cam was not alone. Much more was going on behind the scenes. A reward of £1,000 was offered to the first person to give information leading directly to Martin's arrest, and a similar amount had been offered for the arrest of Harry Roberts, seventeen years earlier, after he went on the run following the murder of three police officers. This information was released to the press at 4 p.m. on that Friday afternoon and it was timed to coincide with the evening's major television bulletins.

From the judicial side of the investigation, Lester Purdy and Peter Enter had been charged with handling the goods stolen by Martin and, having appeared at court, had been remanded in custody for a week. Susie Stephens had been similarly charged; however, she was in a precarious position. She needed help and she got it. She was given bail, her telephone calls were intercepted, twenty-four hour surveillance was carried out on her flat and she was told, quite unequivocally, 'We want Martin on a plate.'

On the Thursday night, she had spoken to Martin on the telephone and agreed to meet him 'at the last place we met' the following night. Martin knew that that was The Milk Churn Restaurant, 70 Heath Street, Hampstead.

Heath Street stretched from north to south, and close by the junction with Hampstead High Street was Hampstead Underground station, on the east footway. The restaurant was situated about fifty yards north of the junction; between restaurant and junction were two side roads, both on the eastern side, Streatley Place and Back Lane, both possible escape routes.

Inside The Milk Churn was a detective inspector from C11, with a female colleague. Initially, the manager Tom Chilton was unaware of the police presence although the clandestine aspect of the observation was spoiled when there was a phone call to the restaurant, which caused Jane Howard, a waitress, to call out, 'Is there a Detective Inspector Tucker, here?'

Long before the meet, Mick Geraghty, wearing a body set (together with other officers) staked out the plot. OPs were set up, one in the Nag's Head public house at 81 Heath Street which overlooked the restaurant. At 5.30 p.m., squad officers had approached the manager Steve Ellis to ask his permission to use a private room upstairs. 'They didn't tell us why they were there and we didn't ask,' said the manager's wife Christine. The pub was designated OP 1.

Inside the premises were Detective Inspector Brightwell, Detective Sergeants Bradley, O'Rourke, Yeoman, Benwell and Burnell, and Detective Constable Chapman; these last three officers were armed. Also present was Detective Constable Francis from Paddington Green police station, who knew Martin well.

A second OP was set up at Kingswell Flats at 58 Heath Street. This was situated south of the restaurant and on the same side of the road but a curve in the road would permit the watchers there to see both the front of the restaurant and also OP 1. This was manned by Detective Chief Superintendent Brown, Detective Chief Inspector Street, Detective Sergeants Branch and Suckling and Detective Constable Gallagher. These last three were armed.

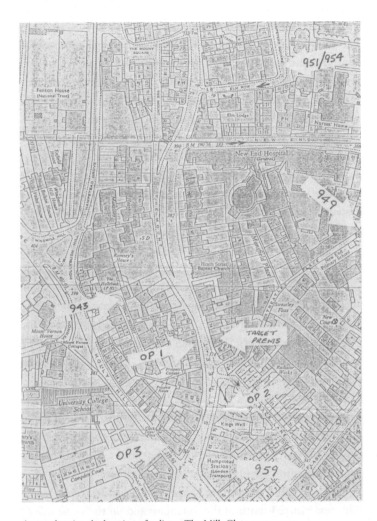

A map showing the location of police at The Milk Churn restaurant.

In addition, Detective Constables Clarke and Geraghty were present, as was Police Constable Lucas from Paddington Green police station, who, like DC Francis in OP 1, was there for identification purposes.

There was a third OP; this was situated at the Nationwide Building Society premises, right at the junction with Holly Hill and Heath Street. Detective Constable Arnold from Paddington Green was there as was the squad driver, seconded for surveillance purposes, Police Constable Colbourne.

Flying Squad cars were kept well out of the way. Central 959 with Police Constables Neilly and Gould, and Detective Sergeants Wood and Hider (who was armed) was parked just off Hampstead High Street, at Flask Walk at the junction with Back Lane.

Central 943, driven by Police Constable Sutherland, with Detective Sergeant Newell and Detective Constable Bryant who were both armed, was parked at Holly Mount at the junction with Hollybush Steps, to the north-west of the restaurant.

Central 949, driven by Police Constable Childs and crewed by Detective Sergeants Miller and Cooke, who were both armed, was parked at the end of Streatley Place Passage in New End; this was to the north-east of the target premises.

To the north of the restaurant, in Hampstead Square at the junction with Elm Row, were two squad vehicles: Central 951, driven by Police Constable Howells and crewed by Detective Inspector Harvey and an armed officer, Detective Constable Walker. Central 954, driven by Police Constable Freeman, contained me, Detective Sergeant Redgrave (armed) and Detective Constable Holloway. From this position, either or both vehicles could swing south into Heath Street.

Four more squad vehicles were parked up: Central 942 and Central 809 in Jack Straw's Castle car park, and Central 801 and Central 944 in Maresfield at the junction with Netherall Gardens.

At the briefing, all this was explained by a senior officer. It seemed fine to me, except for one thing. I remembered how Martin had got away from me ten years previously, via Upton Park Underground station. 'Guv'nor,' I said. 'There's no one covering the route to Hampstead Underground station. If he gets through, he can go straight down the unders and we'll have lost him.'

The senior officer sighed theatrically, as if to say, 'There's always got to be one, hasn't there?' Wearily, he replied, 'Dick, once he's outside the restaurant, he's bollocksed. He's had it. There's enough of us to eat him. You follow?'

I shrugged my shoulders and sat down. One or two sycophantic officers rolled their eyes at this bit of self-centred stupidity in an effort to ingratiate themselves and I heard someone mutter, 'Mr Thicko!'

So there you had it: thirty-five officers, thirteen of them armed, nine Flying Squad cars plus an unspecified number of C11 personnel and vehicles, secreting themselves in and around a very small area – all for the arrest of one man. A tad excessive? A bit over the top? Don't you believe it!

During this tense time, a little light humour evolved, about a mile away. Detective Constable Gordon Harrison and another officer were manning the OP – a flat above the NatWest Bank – opposite Susie Stephens's flat. This was necessary since Martin could of course pay a visit to the premises at any time. There were two twelve-hour shifts and at 7 p.m. Harrison's tour of duty had finished and he and his companion were relieved by two other officers.

Telling the two new officers that they would stay in the area to savour the moment when Martin was arrested, they stated they would adjourn to a nearby pub and return later and, because of the security involved, locked the bank's door on the two fresh observers.

However, Harrison then decided that the pub which they intended to visit was too close to Stephens's flat so he and his companion wandered off to another pub in Hampstead where they enjoyed a little refreshment, became engrossed in their conversation and lost track of time.

By the time they returned, matters had taken a decisive turn of events. 'We returned to the OP to find two very irate colleagues who were pretty pissed off,' Harrison told me. They had had to shout, through the bank door's letterbox to a passer-by, to request that he enter the pub which they believed Harrison and partner had entered and to see if two men fitting their descriptions were ensconced therein and if that were the case, to ask them to return immediately. 'I often wonder what that member of the public thought about someone shouting through a letterbox from what they would believe to be inside a bank, at 9 p.m.!' Harrison wryly told me.

While Harrison and his partner were indulging in the type of light refreshment that a mile away to the east thirty-five of their fellow Flying Squad contemporaries were dreaming of, matters were rather taut as all of us got into position – and we waited. And then a thought occurred to me. No one had given consideration to Martin intercepting police radio transmissions. Criminals, especially armed robbers, were using monitoring devices, such as the 'Bearcat' range, more and more. Among the enormous amount of property stolen from Eurotell Security Specialists the previous March, had that included monitoring equipment? Of course, much – but not all – of that equipment had been retrieved after the raid on the basement flat at Ladbroke Grove almost a week previously but then again might Martin have held on to just one such piece of equipment for just this type of eventuality?

Well, if he had, it was too late now. And after about an hour, at 7.40 p.m., the radio crackled into life. 'All units, stand by ... all units from OP3, a brown Sierra entering the plot, towards the target premises – Index: Bravo, Yankee, Golf, seven, eight-er, zero, Yankee.'

'That's the one!' I whispered excitedly.

'It may not be,' said Tony Freeman doubtfully.

'It is! That's the index number that Cam came up with!' I hissed. 'That's Martin!'

I wonder why we were talking in whispers? Probably because by now we were convinced that Martin possessed some supernatural powers whereby he could overhear whispered conversations a couple of hundred yards away – that's how this job gripped us!

Yes, Martin it certainly was; he drove through the plot and parked the car in a small car park, right next to a C11 vehicle. Through his body set, Mick Geraghty could hear the car's female C11 occupant whispering her information to the team. Martin got out of the Sierra and strolled down Heath Street to the restaurant, where he looked inside. Susie Stephens was not there so he continued walking down the thoroughfare. He was positively identified by Jim Francis, one of the watchers inside the Nag's Head, who passed this information on to OP2; in fact, he passed so close to Tony Yeoman, who was also in the pub, 'I could've reached out and touched him!' he told me, 'but I was awaiting the attack call. Then suddenly Don Brown stepped out of his OP, tried a textbook training school-type arrest, missed, and Martin was off.' The attack call from the OP came too late, or the radio was defective or it wasn't given at all, but for whatever reason, Martin darted down the hill. There was nowhere else for him to go; he had passed the two side turnings so dodging the cars Martin dashed straight into Hampstead Underground station, where, of course, nobody was waiting to intercept him. It's likely that the officers in the OP were the only ones who had heard the vocal attack command; they rushed out into the street and the other officers on the observation saw them. This was no time for me to say 'I told you so!' and we emerged from our hiding places and roared down Heath Street after him.

Hampstead Underground station from the ticket hall down to the platforms is 183 feet, making it the deepest station in London. There are four lifts down to the platforms but Martin disregarded them, as we did. Both Martin and pursuers chose the spiral staircase containing 320 steps.

To the astonishment of Charles Wehner from Queen's Park, West London, he saw, 'at least twelve armed men' burst into the station's ticket hall. 'They were all carrying pistols,' he said, 'and they raced down the escalators [*sic*] to the platforms.'

'We got the buzz from the first OP,' Alan Branch told me, 'but the attack wasn't given. I ran after Martin and I could almost touch him, but I was lumbered by wearing a bullet-proof vest. I was just in front of Don Brown and as we ran down the spiral staircase, I ricked my ankle but I didn't feel it at the time because of the rush of adrenaline.'

'I never saw anybody run so fast,' commented Tony Yeoman, no slouch himself.

'As he got to the station, I nearly grabbed him, but he was quicker,' recalled Mick Geraghty. 'He leapt the first straight stairs in one leap. I was the first after him. We both ran down the circular steps but at the bottom, he was about ten yards ahead of me and turned right on to a platform. He ran towards a tunnel and as he entered, a train came in. I shouted at the travellers and told the train driver not to move off. I told him to get the power off on that line.'

'I don't know how many stairs there are, but there are a lot!' remembered Gerry Gallagher who ran into the station with Tony Yeoman. 'I tripped and rolled down the last dozen or so. By the time we got to the platform, a train had pulled in and by now Tony and I were joined by Nicky Benwell and Tom Bradley. There was no sign of Martin and as passengers were getting off the train, we were shouting at them to get back on. There was a bit of screaming and shouting as I was in plain clothes, waving a gun and shouting, in a broad Northern Ireland accent, "get back on the train, get back on the train!" Nicky Benwell told me later that many passengers thought it was the IRA hijacking the train, as they could only hear me roaring like a bull. Nicky walked the length of the train, explaining to everyone what was happening: he even got a round of applause. The train guard was useless and it was a young boy who told us that Martin had gone down the tunnel, squeezing between the end of the train carriage and the tunnel wall.'

Detective Constable Mark Bryant was another of the officers who, gun drawn, searched the train. 'A left-wing woman stood up and shouted, "You can't do this!",' recalled Bryant. 'A black member of London Transport witnessed the altercation. "Quiet, woman!" he thundered. "Sit down! I'se working with the po-lice!"'

Alan Branch had also heard what the boy had said; he and Detective Sergeant 'Nobby' Clarke went to enter the tunnel which led southbound, towards Belsize Park Underground station but at that moment a train arrived at the station. Branch could see Martin's silhouette in the lights of the train. After the train had left, both officers entered the tunnel and discovered there was a connection which led into the northbound tunnel; unbeknown to them Martin had discovered this too.

Mick Geraghty was seriously out of breath and walked over to the northbound tunnel mouth and sat down. 'John Redgrave came up to me and gave me his gun, saying the radios didn't work and there were problems with communicating up top. I stayed getting my breath back when I heard a noise in the tunnel. As I turned, I saw Martin approaching me from the tunnel.'

Martin had doubled back through the connecting tunnel, doubtlessly hoping to lose himself in the embarking passengers from the train which had already been checked by the squad officers. 'I pointed the gun at him and shouted "armed police!",' said Geraghty. 'He stopped, looked at the gun and turned and ran. I shouted after him, then turned and shouted to the arrest team, "He's here!"'

Martin had ducked back once more through the recess and into the southbound tunnel; he was now running towards Belsize Park Underground station, three-quarters of a mile away. If he could outpace his pursuers; if he was not electrocuted; if he was not run down by a tube train – if, if, if – then it was quite possible that once more, he would have outwitted the police and added another chapter to his ever-expanding escape CV.

Capture in the Tunnel

The most senior officer present was Detective Chief Superintendent Don Brown. At the time, he was two months away from his 50th birthday and in his twenty-ninth year of service. This was his third tour with the Flying Squad; during his first, twelve years earlier, he had been commended by the commissioner for performing secret and dangerous work in Northern Ireland and eighteen months later gained another for courage in arresting a gang of robbers.

The years had not dissipated his bravery; shouting for the current to be switched off, he jumped down into the tunnel and set off, in pursuit of Martin. He was followed by Nicky Benwell, Davy Walker and other officers. Steve Holloway recalls the late Detective Sergeant Graham Newell grabbing a London Transport employee by the throat because he was dithering about contacting his control room to have the power turned off.

In an emergency situation, as indeed this was, the station staff would contact the the Northern Line Traffic Controller at Euston to shut off the potentially lethal traction current – 600 volts DC – who in turn would contact the station staff at Belsize Park or train crews in the affected area. In fact, it appears that the current was not immediately switched off, because when this is done, the emergency lighting automatically comes on in the tunnel; but none did either at Hampstead or Belsize Park.

And of course, neither Don Brown nor any of the other intrepid officers were aware that the four-foot-eight-and-a-half-inch-wide track was still 'live' as they made their way through the gloom of the twelve-foot diameter tunnel in pursuit of London's most dangerous criminal towards Belsize Park.

Meanwhile, Fred Arnold who had witnessed Martin's arrival – and then his departure – from OP3 was tasked to patrol between the two tube stations. This was because it was feared that Martin might escape through one of the shafts containing ventilator fans to remove hot air from the tunnels, which were covered with manhole covers in the roadways.

Being part of the tide of officers rushing down that circular staircase was very much like being immersed in a sink where the plug had just been released and now the water was swirling into the waste pipe. By the time I reached the platform, my heart was beating so fast that if it had suddenly popped out of my mouth and rolled around at my feet I shouldn't have been particularly surprised. If I had been told to follow the officers into the tunnel, of course, I would have had to go; but when I was directed to get down to Belsize Park, to cut off Martin's escape, I must admit to experiencing a feeling of relief.

Steve Holloway and Gerry Gallagher were two more of several other officers directed to get back up to Hampstead High Street and go to Belsize Park Underground station, which compared with Hampstead was a mere 119 feet below street level. It would, of course, have been much easier to use the radios to alert the remaining officers who were outside the station of the current situation but because we were so far underground the radios simply could not transmit or receive. It is a situation which, to date, has never been rectified.

I was still unaware of the existence of the lifts at the station, so I wearily plodded my way, back up those rotten 320 stairs. Alfie

Howells was the remaining squad driver left, so together we set off for Belsize Park.

Meanwhile, Alan Branch and 'Nobby' Clarke were in the tunnel, following the other officers. 'We were checking every recess in the tunnel,' Branch told me. 'It was pitch-black down there.' At some stage, the power was shut off because one of the pursing officers later said, 'There were dim lights in the tunnel' and this, of course, was the emergency lighting. It had also brought the southbound train, which had just left Hampstead station, to a halt. Don Brown and the other officers entered the train via the guard's door; Sarah Thompson, a 27-year-old civil servant recalled, 'Police ran from carriage to carriage shouting "Armed police – stay where you are!" Later, we had to walk through the tunnel by police and London Transport workers to Hampstead station.' Michael White, also 27 and a passenger on the stranded train said, 'The carriage was in semi-darkness. Everybody remained very calm – they all thought the system had broken down again. Then after about twenty minutes, three armed policemen with guns in their hands burst through the carriages. They shouted "armed police – nobody move!" Then other police followed, all in plain clothes.' Carol Vince of Edgware also recounted the police officers invading the carriages and added, 'They went through on to the tracks but came back a short time later to announce, "We've got the guy we were looking for."'

By now, police, some with dogs, were arriving outside Belsize Park Underground station, as were large numbers of pedestrians who were told to get to the other side of the road: 'He may have a gun,' they were told by the officers.

Paul Sanderson, a cinema worker, was in the station forecourt when police cars screeched to a halt. 'Men with guns started to run into the station,' he said. 'We stood back amazed at the confusion and the shouting. It all happened so quickly.'

Meanwhile, Peter Brod, a 31-year-old BBC radio producer had just arrived at the station and had ascended in the lift to street level, to dine with friends. 'When I got out of the lift, there were several armed detectives and uniformed men. One plain clothes man had a drawn pistol and was shouting, "Get out! Get out!",' he recalled, adding, 'they seemed very tense!'

Down on the platform, Margaret Owen, a 24-year-old civil servant, was sitting on a bench waiting for the train to take her home. 'There was only one man on the platform with me,' she said. 'Suddenly, this detective came rushing down the steps and told us to get off the platform and out of the station as quickly as possible. Then he hurried along the platform. A few seconds later, I saw him flinging a youngish man in jeans against the wall. The man was pressed up against the wall with his hands above him. He didn't seem to struggle and I didn't see any guns. Then I ran as fast as I could.'

It was quickly ascertained that the young man was not Martin and upon being unpeeled from the wall, was dusted down and allowed to go on his way.

'When I got to Belsize Park, I was joined by a DS called Billy Miller,' recalled Gerry Gallagher. 'Billy and I went down to the southbound platform. I recall the brilliantly lit platform area and the overwhelming silence. I was aware that I couldn't see into the tunnel and equally aware that anyone exiting the tunnel towards the platform could easily see me. Billy stood with his back to the tunnel wall exit and I grabbed a red fire bucket, full of sand and dog-ends, put it on the platform near the edge and got down behind it. I was shitting myself. I had my gun out resting on the lip of the bucket, pointing at the tunnel. After what appeared to be a lifetime, I heard Nicky Benwell's voice coming from the tunnel. I initially thought they had lost Martin but then I clearly heard him say, "Detective Sergeant Benwell, coming out with a prisoner" and Nicky came out of the tunnel with little Dave Walker, another C8 guy who had a "seek & search" style lamp with him. They'd found Martin in a small recessed area, no more than a couple of feet wide along the length of the tunnel wall.'

Further back in the tunnel, Alan Branch saw Martin arrested. 'He wouldn't put his hands up,' he told me.

Billy Miller recalls being at the end of the platform at Belsize Park when he decided to relieve himself. Just as he was about to do so, he saw Martin approaching from twenty feet away and drew his police issue revolver. Martin stopped in his tracks and it was debateable which of the protuberances held in Miller's hands caused him the most consternation. As he remarked to me over thirty years later, 'Good job I needed a slash, eh?'

Martin, dressed in a dark jacket and shirt and casual trousers, with a mixture of dirt and grease on his face, had been arrested at 8.43 p.m. 'Take it easy, guys, you've got me,' he said, and after thirty-four days on the run, they had.

Ten-year-old Jude Campbell had been out rollerskating near his home in Belsize Park and saw Martin being escorted from the station. 'He looked very scared and nervous,' said Jude. 'He was walking slowly. I couldn't see whether he was handcuffed because of the policeman so close around him. They put him in a red Ford and drove away very fast with the sirens wailing. To think I was looking at Martin's picture only this morning,' he added. 'It was on a poster outside Hampstead police station. I never thought I was going to see him arrested tonight!'

Police Constable John Barnie was driving the local area car and was told to cover the exit from Belsize Park station. He and his RT operator PC Kevin Rose were besieged by the press demanding information regarding Martin's arrest but they were unable to assist. A London Transport employee had chalked up 'Station closed until further notice' on a blackboard outside the station; fed up with the persistence of the press, Barnie borrowed a piece of chalk and added: 'PS. Martin's bin nicked!'

Safely contained in the back of Tom Renshaw's squad car, Martin was taken to Paddington Green police station, where he was thoroughly searched. He did not have a firearm in his possession but he did have two knives, a bottle of ammonia, pick locks concealed in his hair and when Davy Walker noticed that Martin had problems speaking, he told him to open his mouth. When Martin demurred, Walker took the simple expedient of pinching his nostrils together, which had the desired effect. Stuck to the roof of his mouth with chewing gum was a tiny Swiss Army multi-purpose penknife. Ruefully Martin told the officers, 'You've got to cover all angles, haven't you? You can't blame me for trying.'

By the time I made my way down to the platform at Belsize Park, it was deserted. 'They're all gorn, mate,' said a passing London Transport employee. So I made my way up the stairs, once more and Alfie drove me to Paddington Green. There, in the charge room, I saw for the second and last time the man I had started hunting ten years previously. We had never spoken to each other and now we never would. He was sitting on a bench, looking slightly dishevelled but relaxed. Martin caught my glance; he looked up at me. I wanted to see if I could detect even a flicker of recognition in his eyes, but there was nothing; just disinterest and he looked away. 'Ten bloody years!' I thought, 'and still I didn't catch you!'

But what did my pricked vanity matter? Martin had been arrested, by whom it mattered not, and one dangerous member of society was out of circulation and that was the most important thing. That and my desire for a large drink, the first in fourteen days. As Gerry Gallagher recalled, 'In true Flying Squad style, we all adjourned to the Green Man pub just around the corner from Paddington Green.'

The seventeeth-century Green Man pub at 308 Edgware Road was suddenly flooded with extremely thirsty squad officers and as the hour reached midnight, Gordon Harrison recalled the licensee demanding to know who would be accountable for the after-hours drinking. An officer asked for pen and paper and, as Harrison recalled, 'After writing on it, handed it to the licensee and told him to place it on the window of the door.' After reading the note, the landlord proudly positioned it in the window as requested. It read: 'I authorise this public house to remain open to officers of the Flying Squad until further notice – signed by the commander.' The signature was quite unlike Frank Cater's which led many to believe that he may not have been the authentic signatory to that profligate document.

'Much later that night and after a few celebratory drinks,' as Flying Squad driver Tom Renshaw remembered, 'I took DI Tony Brightwell home, where his wife told me that the following morning, he stood at the top of the stairs and shouted "We've got him!"'

Not only did this make headline television news that night, the popular crime television programme *The Gentle Touch* was interrupted to inform the viewers of Martin's arrest. When I arrived home – I was, I believe a little unsteady on my feet – it was to loud acclamation from the Kirby clan. Colourful greeting cards were in abundance and one from my 11-year-old daughter Barbara with the heading 'Happy Families' read as follows:

I will tell you a story. On a Friday night, some of the Kirby family were watching TV. The Gentle Touch was on. Sue, Mum, Robert and Barbara were watching it. The adverts came on, then a newsflash came on. The newsreader said David Martin had been caught. He was chased by policemen. Everyone cheered, screamed and hugged each other. Then Sue said, 'Get out the drinks and have a toast to Dad.' The end.

I doubt by that time I could have consumed one more cubic centilitre of liquid, alcoholic or not!

The next day, the newspapers were full of it, both at home and abroad, with Oregon's *Eugene Register-Guard* laconically noting, 'Scotland Yard gets its man on fourth try.' Homegrown publications were rather more flattering in their comments. 'Martin arrested!' proclaimed the *Daily Mail*. 'Martin caught in tube tunnel!' cried *The Sun*. 'Captured!' shouted the *Daily Express*. Steven Waldorf, who had been 'overwhelmed' by the cards and messages from well-wishers, heard the news while he was still recovering in the Charles Kingsley Ward at St Stephen's Hospital, saying he was relieved to hear of it and that now he wanted to 'fade into the background'. The commissioner sighed with relief. Martin had been recaptured without a shot being fired. It was fortunate that the detectives were all right as well, of course. The hundreds of 'wanted' posters for Martin, which had been prepared and were ready for distribution on the morning of Monday 31 January, were not pulped but were put to one side – just in case of any unexpected eventuality.

But Martin was not done and dusted just yet. Before we leave him in his cell at Paddington, this is what Gordon Harrison recalled:

> I remember going to look at Martin through the wicket gate in his cell and he was one very cool, dispassionate guy, prowling his cell and you got the feeling that he was already planning and plotting what he could do to either escape or evade justice.

Martin had a few other tricks up his sleeve and he would reserve them for the courtroom.

Martin – Centre Stage

artin was interviewed by Detective Inspector Tony Brightwell and Nicky Benwell; the latter later told me 'it was an interesting experience'. Nicky, a member of 10 Squad, had a nice, relaxed manner when dealing with people, criminal or otherwise. On one occasion, having received an absolute paucity of information to such an extent that no sane magistrate would ever have been induced to issue a search warrant and believing this was a no-hoper if ever there was one, he simply knocked on the suspect's front door. When it was opened, Nicky, in his public school accent, politely said to the occupier, 'Good morning. Sergeant Benwell from the Flying Squad. Whereabouts are the guns, please?' To his astonishment, the householder replied, 'You'd better come in – they're under the bed.' It led to the seizure of a whole range of weapons, plus a series of arrests for conspiracy to rob which resulted in Nicky adding another commissioner's commendation to an already growing pile.

Now he interviewed Martin who, referring to his arrest, said, 'Believe me, I did not have a gun. It would not have been so easy for you if I had one.' Asked if that meant he would have fired, Martin replied, 'For sure. You were pointing guns at me, weren't you?'

The officers wanted to know the whereabouts of the five missing guns, to which Martin replied, 'As far as I'm concerned,

I never trusted that list I was shown last time. I want to help you as much as I can. I will tell you everything I've been doing. There were two other guns – a magnum and a target .22. I've put them out to someone but I'm not involving anyone else. They're locked away – that must give you a clue.'

Martin was doing what he did best, goading the police by showing how clever he was. He was telling them things that he was certain they knew nothing about; then he could surprise them by generously providing them with the answer.

As he did in this case: he told the officers to try a security box at Harrods department store under the name of 'Smith'. The interviewers expressed some scepticism at that, but Martin insisted, 'No, really. I'm not saying they're still there, but they were. If you get me a diary, I'll show you the week they were put in.' When the box was identified, searched and found to be empty, Martin simply shrugged and replied, 'I told you I wasn't sure.' So it appears highly likely that although several handguns were still outstanding, Martin did not have immediate access to them and this was partially confirmed by his next set of admissions.

He admitted two burglaries while he was on the run; one was between 21 and 24 January when he broke into Teesdale Publishing, Standard House, Bonhill Street, EC1 and stole photographic equipment valued at £6,721 belonging to John Dunbar – property stolen from that company was found in the stolen Ford Sierra – and the second burglary was at the offices of *Guns Review* in Shoreditch. Martin had scoured the pages of gun magazines, and also *Exchange & Mart*, for people who had guns to sell. He found them; but their only point of contact was a box number, which was housed at *Guns Review*'s office, hence the reason for this burglary. Having broken in and acquired the details of the gun sellers, he photographed their addresses, one in Stevenage, Hertfordshire and another in Osterley, West London.

These photographs were contained in a spool of film in a camera stolen from Teesdale's, at a flat above Bottoms Up off-licence in Notting Hill Gate where Martin admitted living. He had moved in a week before his arrest; it was a complete and utter dump. Neighbours thought squatters had moved in. One woman living opposite noticed that the curtains were drawn and that a light was on at night. Mail and circulars littered the floor, as did Wimpy Burger cartons and paper coffee cups. If Martin had acquired his sustenance from the nearby Wimpy takeaway, no one had noticed him. 'The counter staff serve several people at once,' commented the manager. 'They hear the order, shout it up, hand it over and take the money. They don't have time to study faces.' Unnoticed, living in a room where an old beige sofa, dusty green curtains and a filthy green carpet complemented the wall-to-wall squalor of the premises, for someone who had seen himself as a modern-day Raffles, this was a consummate fall from grace. Enormous faeces floated on top of a filthy, limescale-encrusted lavatory. Perhaps it was Martin's way of welcoming any unannounced visitors and at the same time displaying his contempt for them.

Martin told the officers he wanted to acquire guns 'because I was unarmed and the people looking for me would be armed'. Asked if he wanted the guns for robberies, he replied, 'No, for defence, in case someone came up to me.'

He was asked how many guns he had and Martin, referring to the burglary at the Covent Garden gunsmiths, replied, 'At that time, I had loads of guns. I don't know how many. Listen, I'll give you an example. I found one in the car I didn't even know I had.

I nearly had a fit when I saw it. I certainly haven't got any now. I took as many guns as I could carry. Can you imagine how heavy they were?'

Referring to his attempted arrest at Colour Film Services the previous August, he told the interviewing officers, 'The last time I was nicked, I could have blown them away. They were dead men. The reason I didn't was they were unarmed and if I chopped them, people would have thought I was some sort of an animal.' It was as though Martin was giving himself absolution, through no fault of his own, for not murdering PC Carr. At the conclusion of the interview, Martin said, 'I would just like to say I had no intention of hurting anybody and at no time have I been armed since my escape.' Martin was charged with fourteen offences of robbery, burglary, firearms offences and attempting to murder PC Carr.

Alan Berriman was a career CID officer who, together with many others, had suffered under Sir Robert Mark's despotic 'interchange' dictum and now, upon promotion as Police Sergeant 40 'D', he was stationed at Paddington Green. Coincidentally, he had also been present at Marylebone police station when Peter Finch had been issued with his firearm; now, as station officer, he personally supervised safety and suicide visits to the cells, the consumption of meals by Martin and arranged four-hourly visits by the divisional surgeon. 'Casual conversation with him was kept to a minimum to try to prevent allegations by him,' he told me. 'Everybody was very keyed up to ensure there was no chance of an acquittal on a procedural technicality. As I recall, he was resentful of detention and the divisional surgeon's examinations, even though it was for his benefit. He displayed contempt for everybody.'

There were two court appearances on Monday 31 January. Martin made his first appearance at Marlborough Street Magistrates' Court and Stephens, Purdy and Enter appeared at

Marylebone Magistrates' Court. I'd taken the day off, so when I saw the one o'clock news, I was a little surprised to discover that Acting Detective Inspector Richard Kirby had told the court that he had no objection to bail and that the three defendants were duly remanded until 14 March.

The following day, I mentioned my concerns to Tony Freeman at being in two different places at the same time. 'Oh, that,' he nonchalantly replied. 'One of the press blokes asked who the officer was in the witness box, so I said it was you. Gave you a leg-up, like.'

'Ah. Right,' I said. I didn't understand Tony's reasoning then, any more than I do now!

At Martin's court appearance, the interior of Marlborough Street court was ringed with detectives, with a detective handcuffed to Martin in the dock who had, of course, dressed for the occasion: a grey pullover casually draped over his shoulders, wearing a grey shirt and grey-striped trousers. Detective Chief Superintendent Don Brown asked for a remand in custody for eight days. A girl in the public gallery, dressed in a fur jacket, whined, 'Lies, lies!' rushed out of the court, refused to identify herself and continued to chant, 'It's lies, all lies!'

Meanwhile, the magistrate, Mr St John-Harmsworth – who once famously told a girl, charged with soliciting prostitution, 'Young women who stop men in cars in Hyde Park often come to a sticky end!' – remanded Martin in custody for the specified time. However, outside the court his solicitor, Anthony Blok, stated, 'He told me this morning that he is deeply distressed at not being able to see Miss Susan Stephens, despite promises which he says were made to him by the police. He says he won't eat or drink until he is allowed to see her.'

So there! However, a Scotland Yard spokesperson denied that such a promise had been given, saying, 'Whether a police prisoner is allowed visitors is a matter for the officer in charge. In view of all the circumstances of the Martin case, it was decided he would not be allowed to see any visitors.'

It was pretty sound reasoning. It is quite possible that at that time Martin had formed the view that Stephens was responsible for his incarceration, in which case it would have been injudicious at the very least to have permitted a meeting between them; it was similarly possible that Stephens simply did not wish to see Martin.

Blok also said, 'There has been much public comment about matters not related to the charges faced by my client. Accordingly, he would like the following to be known: he considers he is greatly indebted to Steven Waldorf, whom he has never met. But for what happened to Mr Waldorf, Mr Martin is convinced he would have been shot in the course of his arrest. It should be noted and emphasised that he was unarmed at the time of his arrest. He tells me that at no time whilst at liberty was he in possession of any firearm and as far as I am aware, the police have no evidence to indicate to the contrary.'

Detective Constable Mark Bryant was one of the escorts detailed to convey Martin from Brixton prison to court and back again. There was an altercation between the two after Martin objected to being handcuffed. Bryant, who four years earlier had been highly commended by the commissioner after being injured saving a mentally ill man from falling from a bridge on to live railway lines, was a keep-fit enthusiast, an army reservist and a pretty tough character and managed to disabuse Martin of his notions. 'When I put the handcuffs on him, I couldn't feel a pulse, he was cold, unblinking, wouldn't speak,' Bryant told me. But from these inauspicious beginnings, Martin did appear to thaw. One morning, Bryant offered him a Polo peppermint which Martin accepted and the two men began chatting. Referring to the escape from Marlborough Street Magistrates' Court, Bryant asked, 'How'd you get out of that cell, mate?'

Martin laughed. 'I wouldn't even grass you lot up,' he replied. It was a typical Martin retort; implying mistakes on the part of the police while displaying his own unshakable code of honour.

This was evident at a further hearing at the Magistrates' Court, when Martin asked for reporting restrictions to be lifted and told the magistrate – and, of course, the press – 'It's been suggested that Sue Stephens could be the cause of my present situation.' He added, 'I want to make it absolutely clear that she is in no way to blame.'

Also in court was a young woman, who may or may not have been the person who appeared in the public gallery on the previous occasion, who identified herself as 'Natasha'. Weeping noisily, she called out, 'I've got fags for you but they won't let me see you,' and an attempt to pass both cigarettes and cash to Martin was promptly halted. Outside the court, she told reporters, 'I've tried to see David four times in the last eight days but they won't let me. David helped me when I had money and a prescription stolen. He helped me through a bad time in my life.' This helpfulness on Martin's part may also have been the case with regards to an acquaintance who was a homosexual lorry driver. Apparently, he and Martin had shared an interest in yoga, wholefoods and the occult while the driver was waiting for a sex-change operation.

As it can be well imagined, security was very robust both for Martin's arrival and departure at court; the arrival coincided with a rather unpleasant allegation of police misconduct. Three police cars, two Rovers and a Fiat accompanied Martin's prison van to court but as they arrived and reversed into the yard of the court, it was alleged that there was altercation between the accompanying detectives and the waiting press photographers. Possibly the cause was the Rover, which was following the van and reversed into the Fiat, but it appeared there was a bad-tempered exchange in which it was said that cameras were smashed and newsmen were threatened and knocked over. Pointing to a hole in the road, caused by roadworks, one officer supposedly told a photographer that he would 'fill the hole in with a few of us if we did not move back' and another stated, 'The police accused us of being animals. There was a hell of a scrap involving about a dozen policemen and ten of us. Punches were thrown by the police. It was general harassment.'

The ubiquitous Scotland Yard spokesman stated: 'Any complaint about police behaviour towards photographers will certainly be investigated.'

And so it was. Several days went by and then a senior officer told us, 'Right, a DCI's coming tomorrow to interview you lot about that complaint.' This was the first I'd heard of a complaint, so I replied, 'What complaint's this, then?'

This spineless senior officer simply sighed and rolled his eyes and fixed me with the sort of expression adopted by unkind parents and reserved for a dim-witted child who has failed a simple intelligence test, as if to say, 'You know *exactly* what I'm talking about.' The reason for his recalcitrance was this: he felt that if he were to explain the complaint in detail, it might rebound on him to suggest that he knew all about it and therefore he would in some way be accountable.

I was annoyed and it showed. 'I've got no idea what complaint you're talking about,' I snapped and he grudgingly gave me the bare details. This was the first time I'd heard of it. In fact, it had been reported in a couple of newspapers but I was unaware of it. Nobody had mentioned it to me and of course, at the time of it happening, I was lolling about at home. Still, now I knew about the bare bones of the case, it did strike me as being rather odd.

The press had given us pretty good coverage about the case – not about the shooting of Waldorf of course, but then we hadn't been involved in that aspect of the investigation. But we'd come out of the arrest of Martin smelling of roses, so why would any of us want to have what appeared to be a confrontation with the press? It didn't make sense.

The following day, the chief inspector arrived, with a detective sergeant as his bag-carrier, whom I shall refer to simply as 'Trevor'. In common with the whole of the Metropolitan Police Force, I detested him. He had the ability to get under anybody's skin, just by a look or a word; within seconds he could transform the mildest-mannered soul into an infuriated psychopath. This had happened with a CID typist who was known for her sunny, outgoing, placid temperament – in fact, she practised yoga to preserve her tranquillity. It took just the blinking of an eyelid for Trevor to seriously upset her and for her to pick up a metal tray, full of mugs of tea and smash him over the head with it. Staggering around the office with blood running down his face, Trevor looked a pitiful sight and the officers who were present immediately expressed profound concern; for the typist, that is, not Trevor, who was ignored and permitted to bleed, quite copiously.

So the chief inspector cautioned me and proceeded with his questioning; I told him that I was not present at the alleged fracas, did not know who had been, and had heard nothing about the supposed incident. Trevor wrote the notes containing my unhelpful replies which I signed as being correct. I left the office and promptly forgot all about the matter about which I knew nothing in the first place; that is, until a couple of weeks later.

In the meantime, I had a great deal to be getting on with. Although the Martin investigation had only occupied me for a couple of weeks, I had a large backlog of work to contend with, which until now had had to be placed on the backburner, plus more work coming in. The Metropolitan Police Solicitors' Department was understandably getting a bit shirty because they hadn't received any documentation from me in respect of the 'Eric' case, so that report had to be addressed as a matter of urgency. There were other reports to be submitted as well, plus disposal of property and the thousand-and-one other matters which took up a Flying Squad officer's life. There was also a number of people who demanded my attention; one was a well-known 'key man' – not one of Martin's standing, but pretty close, nonetheless – who, without any further discourse, I wanted to put on the sheet for conspiracy to burgle safety deposit boxes in Mayfair and then follow this up with a more leisurely discussion about his involvement in a high-value burglary in Knightsbridge. At the other end of the criminal social scale, there was a yob from a Barking council estate who required an interview regarding a conspiracy to rob in Hendon and also, I needed to know the whereabouts of a young man from Dalston, in respect of possessing a gun. This trio was well aware that I was after them and the fact that I hadn't made any overt moves in their respective directions for a couple of weeks must have made them think they were home and dry. To disabuse them of this notion, I needed to crank up some informants, with the promise of a handsome bursary from the Yard's informants' fund if they were successful in housing these three and a kick up the arse if they were not.

It was a few weeks later that Trevor telephoned me. Because this internal investigation had gone nowhere – no one it seemed knew anything – it appeared that this had become a source of annoyance to the chief inspector who was now allegedly threatening havoc, by returning to check everybody's mileage claims, refreshment expenses, etc. All this, said Trevor, could be avoided if I were simply to provide him with the names of the guilty parties and as I began to gibber with rage at this infamous suggestion, he hung up. Trevor obviously hadn't learnt a lesson from the tray-wielding typist! He never did phone back, which saved him from receiving an earful of blasphemous filth from me. But there you are: a small, unpleasant episode in a busy Flying Squad officer's life. Rather more was going on in David Martin's life, because on 14 March 1983, he appeared at Lambeth Magistrates' Court, London's top security court, for committal to the Old Bailey.

It appeared that Martin had gone off the idea of the hunger strike and also Miss Stephens, for the time being at least, because through the dock's bulletproof screen, separating the court from the public gallery, he carried out what the *Glasgow Herald* described as 'an animated conversation' with a girl named 'Natasha'.

David Boyd, representing the Director of Public Prosecutions office, outlined the case, mentioning his threats regarding firearms on the two occasions he had been confronted by police. In a statement, part-read out in court, Detective Inspector Tony Brightwell had asked him, 'Do you know Steven Waldorf, the man who was shot?' Martin had replied, 'No, I don't think I have ever met him. I read somewhere he's a Jew. I would not have met him because I don't like Jews.' This was no more than grandstanding; in fact, one of Martin's associates while he was serving his nine-year sentence had been Jewish.

Anthony Blok once more represented Martin; he made a submission to the magistrate Maurice Guymer that there was insufficient evidence for his client to be committed on the charge of attempting to murder PC Carr. Mr Guymer felt otherwise. In one final attempt to show his contempt for the system, Martin instructed Blok to make an application for bail, saying, 'He feels that if he is granted bail, this will give him a chance to prove to the court that he can and does indeed wish to go straight.' Blok added that as part of his bail conditions, Martin would live with his parents but perhaps Mr Guymer had read Martin's father's comments in the press, in which he exhorted his son to 'keep on running' and with masterly understatement he mildly replied, 'I don't feel that I can, in all the circumstances, grant bail,' and Martin was committed in custody to stand his trial at the Old Bailey.

Anthony Blok seemed a little close to his client; later he got even closer to another client after Blok appeared at Croydon Crown Court on 30 June 2009 and at the age of 72 was sentenced to four years' imprisonment for three counts of money-laundering, perjury and perverting the course of public justice. The matter was referred to the Solicitors Disciplinary Tribunal later that year – he had previously appeared before the tribunal seven years earlier – and they decided that he was not fit to practise as a solicitor again.

The press, perhaps in revenge for their staff and equipment being allegedly knocked about, launched an attack on the Flying Squad, alleging corruption in general and being responsible for the shooting of Steven Waldorf in particular. The Assistant Commissioner (Crime), Gilbert Kelland, who prior to this CID appointment had spent all of his thirty-seven years' service in uniform, hastily checked the facts and when he was more than satisfied that no Flying Squad officer had been present at the shooting in Pembroke Road, he issued a denial, saying in part: 'Following this incident, the task of locating and arresting David Martin (for whom Mr Waldorf had been mistaken) who was wanted for the attempted murder of a policeman was given to the Flying Squad and successfully accomplished on January 28 1983.' According to Kelland's memoirs, the squad was practically in a state of exultant swoon at being exonerated from a situation in which they had never been involved.

So in the judicial process of things, this was the end of round one for Martin. He of course was the subject of twenty-four hour security while he was on remand. Although the evidence had been served on his solicitors, the papers were being checked and rechecked to ensure there were no loose ends. Everything now depended on the strength of the prosecution case, which would commence in six months' time.

Martin's Trial

O n 21 September 1983, Martin's trial commenced at No. 2 Court at the Old Bailey. The no-nonsense judge was Mr Justice Kilner-Brown OBE, TD, who eleven years previously had sentenced Frederick Joseph Sewell, who had shot and murdered Superintendent Gerard Richardson GC during the course of a £106,033 jewel robbery in Blackpool, to thirty years' imprisonment.

Martin performed his usual trick of refusing to plead to the indictment. 'It's not possible to make a plea at the moment,' he said when the first count of the indictment was put to him by the court's chief clerk, Mr Michael McKenzie, and when each of the fourteen remaining counts were put, he answered, 'The same.' The judge ordered that pleas of not guilty were entered. By saying nothing, Martin was tacitly suggesting to an unkind legal world that it should 'do its worst', but given the weight of evidence against him it was just as well that he had the services of Ivan (later, Sir Ivan) Lawrence QC, MP, who led John Caudle, to defend him. Lawrence had defended in over ninety murder trials, and his clients included Ronnie Kray (in both his earlier blackmail trial and the later sensational murder trial) and the mass murderer Dennis Nilsen.

The prosecution was represented by Kenneth (later, His Honour Judge) Richardson QC who led John Nutting (later Sir John Nutting QC) and opened the case for the Crown, detailing all of the crimes with which he had been charged since his release from his nine-year prison sentence. It was also made clear to the jury that although DC Peter Finch was an important part of the case against Martin, he would not be giving evidence since he was soon to go on trial for the attempted murder of Steven Waldorf. Referring to Martin's escape from Marlborough Street Magistrates' Court, Richardson told the court, 'How he escaped, we do not know. When he was asked, he declined to say and perhaps one is not surprised at that.'

Two days later, PC Carr limped into court and told the jury of his near fatal encounter with Martin on the night of 5 August the previous year. After Martin had started to walk towards the door, and he and PC Fretter had closed with him, PC Carr said, 'I grabbed his right arm with both my hands. My right hand went to his wrist and my left hand to his elbow.' Within seconds, a shot rang out, followed by another and Carr realised that Martin was holding a gun. 'Let go, or I'll shoot,' said Martin, but Carr hung on, and told the court, 'I carried on pulling his arm round towards his back, hoping to force the gun out of his hand. There was a third shot. It hit me in the top of the groin. I didn't realise I had been hit. I felt a movement on my hip. Then I felt a wet, warm, sticky dampness down my leg. I carried on fighting with him, hoping to bring the gun under control. I carried on for one or two seconds and my leg gave way. I collapsed backwards and Martin said, "If you move, I'll give you another."'

As PC Carr lay bleeding on the floor, Martin ran down the stairs. 'I placed my right hand on my groin as hard as I could and put my left hand hard on top to try to control the bleeding,' said Carr. 'I believe I managed to stop the flow of blood with my hands.'

Lawrence objected to Carr reading from his notes. A police officer may refer to his notes in court, providing they were 'made at the time or as soon after as reasonably practicable'. Of course, because of his injuries, this was impossible and although the judge ruled that Carr should not be able to refer to his pocketbook, it made little difference. When one is shot at point-blank range by a gun-toting, borderline psychopath, the sequence of events is indelibly imprinted upon one's memory and Carr experienced little difficulty in providing a comprehensive testimony.

Martin's defence barrister insinuated that PC Carr had been shot by accident; however, the evidence suggested otherwise, especially after PC Steven Lucas gave evidence of Martin's arrest the previous 15 September. He stated that Martin and Finch were struggling, and when Martin shouted, 'I'll have you – I'll blow you away,' Lucas added, 'It sounded as if he meant it.' As other officers flooded on to the seventh floor of the block of flats, Lucas said, 'I moved out of their line of fire. The black gun which Martin was holding fell from his grasp on to the floor. Then I saw him produce a silver gun from somewhere. He was holding it in his right hand. I shouted to my colleagues, "He's got a gun!" Then I heard a shot which I believe came from PC Van-Dee. Martin fell to the ground with DC Finch on top of him.'

In cross-examination, Lawrence accused Lucas of not telling the truth as to what had actually happened and suggested that he had given his account as 'an attempt to justify the shooting of Martin – perhaps in a panic'. 'As far as the shooting,' stated Lawrence, 'what actually happened was that Martin came up in the lift, turned right out of the lift and right again into the corridor. He collided with DC Finch and was promptly shot by PC Van-Dee.'

'No, sir,' replied Lucas. 'That is totally untrue.'

Lawrence insinuated that Martin never had time to draw any guns but Lucas firmly replied, 'He drew two guns, sir.'

I spoke to Peter Finch about these allegations over thirty years later. 'When I approached Martin,' he told me, 'I told the young

PC to wait whilst I had a word with "her". I think we were all taking the situation very lightly and were not scared or uptight about it. So there was no ambush.'

Lawrence suggested that Lucas was 'practically lost' without reading from his notes which he had made later that night, but this was bluster, an old chestnut usually seized upon by defence barristers, even those as experienced as Ivan Lawrence. It was effectively countered by PC Lucas stating that they aided his memory so that he could get his account correct.

It was a ploy used again when Bob Cook gave evidence with Lawrence suggesting that he had 'collaborated' with other officers in compiling his notes, the intention being to convey to the jury that it was an improper thing to do. Cook replied that he disliked the term 'collaborated' since it suggested wrong or dishonest practice and that further it was quite permissible under the Judges Rules for officers to confer when writing up notes.

Lawrence was scathing regarding Martin's arrest at Crawford Place, saying that the officers knew in advance full well who he was and acted in a 'laidback' manner in carrying out his arrest. He went further; when officers denied seeing Finch hit Martin with his revolver, he suggested that they were lying on oath. They were not and now is as good a time as any to discredit this suggestion.

When a prisoner was committed for trial the prosecution were obliged to serve all of the pertinent statements on the defence, usually prior to the committal at the Magistrates' Court. The defence, in those days, did not have to provide any details whatsoever of what their defence was likely to be. So in between committal and trial – in Martin's case, just over six months – the defence solicitors and barristers had ample opportunity to pore over the prosecution papers, gleefully noting every inconsistency and adding them all together so that in the quiet and calm of a courtroom, accusations could be bellowed at the police officers. Although Finch would not be giving evidence, nevertheless his statement – in which he admitted hitting Martin with his gun – was served on the defence, together with statements from officers who agreed with Finch's statement.

But when police officers go into life-threatening situations there is no time coolly to assess the situation and then make a dispassionate judgement as to what's happening. Police officers being police officers have to make split-second decisions and concentrate upon what they're doing. Therefore those officers who denied seeing Finch hit Martin did so simply because they did not witness it; they were focusing on restraining the wildly kicking and struggling prisoner.

I too have been in similar situations, once in particular in a bedroom with a man running amok wielding a knife. Even though that bedroom was far smaller than the landing at Crawford Place, when it came to recording our evidence afterwards, there were some things which some officers saw and heard which others did not. All that can be done in those circumstances is simply to say what it was you did see, knowing that in months to come the defence will be making capital out of those inconsistencies. There you are – in the legal minefield of English justice, that's life!

Nicky Benwell gave evidence of Martin's arrest in the tunnel. Telling the jury he told Martin to raise his hands as he walked towards him, he stated that Martin refused to lift his hands up. Later Martin told him, 'That would have been giving into you completely. I could never do that.'

Cross-examining, Lawrence said, 'He was deliberately refusing to obey your order in circumstances where he had some reason to think it not unlikely he would be shot?'

Benwell replied, 'I would agree with that.'

Although the expression 'suicide by cop' was not in general usage at that time, this was precisely what Martin had been attempting. It describes the way in which criminals, unwilling to end their own lives, will put police into the impossible position of having to shoot them so that in that split second, they (the victim) will achieve immortality – or so they think. When the matter of the knife hidden in Martin's mouth was raised, Benwell said, 'I wasn't sure if he had it for suicidal purposes or whether in order to try and make a further escape.'

This closed the case for the prosecution and the weekend intervened. On Monday 3 October, Ivan Lawrence made various submissions and Kenneth Richardson, perhaps surprisingly, told the judge that he had given 'very careful consideration' to the evidence of how PC Carr came to be shot in the groin. Martin had fired not caring particularly where the officer was shot, he said, adding, 'In those circumstances, nobody should complain if a charge of attempted murder was brought. But having said that, if one looks at the reality of the situation, it would seem that the basic intent at that stage would have been much more to escape arrest.' Thus, the charge of attempting to murder PC Carr was dropped.

Now it was Martin's turn to give evidence. Naturally, he was dressed for the part in a blue-and-white striped shirt, brown trousers with a brilliant yellow strip sewn into one leg, and brown leather slippers, trimmed in yellow. Ivan Lawrence would later describe him as possessing 'strikingly handsome, if feminine features', although others would have begged to differ. Martin was the centre of attention in front of a packed spectators' gallery and an even more crowded press bench and for the next day and a half, he would be loving it.

The reason for being at Colour Film Services, said Martin, was to copy videos; he had done so previously, copying twenty at a time. However, this he decided would be his final run; and he had imparted this information to the unnamed gang behind this multi-million pound video piracy scam, who were displeased with him. Therefore, he had brought with him a handgun, purely for protection, in case these evil gangsters came to the office to harm him. Are you with me so far, children? Right. During the struggle with PC Carr, the gun – which had a hair-pressure trigger – went off accidentally, since Martin had no intention of shooting anyone. However, the gun which the police said had been used to shoot PC Carr did not have a hair-pressure trigger. This was a setback, albeit one of little importance: one of the handguns found in Martin's possession when he was arrested six weeks later *did* have a hair-pressure trigger; naturally, said Martin, the police had swapped the two guns over. Apparently the bullet which had been fired could not be found and a great deal of capital was made over this.

The gun which had allegedly been used to shoot PC Carr was passed to the jury for inspection; however, first it was passed to Martin, having ensured it was unloaded. It gave him the perfect opportunity for some more grandstanding, telling the jury, 'It is unloaded, you know; I might blow my head off and make a terrible mess in court.'

Remarks like this were food and drink to the spectators' gallery and the unloaded pistol was passed around and merrily clicked by the jury members, to ensure that it did indeed have a hair-pressure trigger. When one thinks about it, it was the height of folly to have passed the firearm to Martin. He would have known this was going to happen; it would not have been impossible for an associate to have smuggled ammunition to him. In the twinkling of an eye, Martin could have loaded the gun, shot the judge and, in the confusion, escaped. You think that's too far-fetched? Then, with respect, you haven't been following examples of Martin's ingenuity as closely as you might.

When Lawrence put it to him that he had 'in due course, escaped,' Martin replied, 'Well … they lost me, put it that way.' Martin was thoroughly enjoying himself, saying, 'If I shoot myself in the process of being arrested, perhaps that is resisting arrest.'

Regarding the shooting of PC Carr, he was prompted to admit, 'Perhaps I should not have had a gun in my hand,' but his colossal ego necessitated qualifying his remarks with an attempt at justification by adding: 'But it is his fault for actually grabbing hold of my hand and wrenching my arm about.'

Martin told the jury that many years before he had been a photographer and that during late 1982 he had been involved in security work: 'Anything from manufacturing covert listening devices to fitting locks on doors.' Asked by his barrister about the truthfulness of the police evidence regarding how he had been approached as he had got out of the lift and inserted a key in the door of his flat and had been told, 'Excuse me, love,' Martin's reply was immediate: 'The only thing which was said to me, was "bang". It never got any further than that.'

Cross-examined by Richardson, the exchanges between the two became sharper; when asked his reasons for taking five guns out of the country, Richardson was goaded into replying, 'No doubt your criticisms of the lax gun laws in this country will be noted,' but there was also no doubt that Martin was ahead on points.

Because of Martin's allegations of impropriety by the police officers, his character could be put before the jury and his convictions were read out in court. Richardson suggested that because he had spent so many years in prison, he carried guns to shoot his way out of trouble to avoid being returned to prison. He described as 'absolute nonsense' Martin's claim that he carried guns in order to kill himself if the prospect of arrest presented itself. 'The reason why I suggest you were prepared to use guns to evade arrest,' said Richardson, 'was because having been in prison many years, you were not prepared to go back there and were prepared to do anything to avoid it,' claims which Martin denied.

Following the completion of his evidence, the jury was shown photographs of Martin dressed in women's black underwear. This was because during three of the offences carried out by Martin in 1982 he had dressed as a woman. The judge told the jury, 'We are not concerned with this man's private habits. I think it sufficient to show you photographs as corroboration that he might be mistaken for a woman. In other respects he is a perfectly normal man but it is part of his scene that he dresses himself up as a woman.'

In his closing speech, Ivan Lawrence conceded that his client was 'no knight in shining armour' and told the jury, 'I don't mind what you think of him as a person, probably not very much.' However, he suggested that as a result of Martin's past life of crime and now, facing a likely serious sentence, the police might have overreacted in their dealings with him. With the type of punishment likely to follow, having spent nine years in prison, might well lead him to adopt an attitude of 'I couldn't care less, let them shoot me; I want to commit suicide,' said Lawrence.

On 7 October, Mr Justice Kilner-Brown summed up the evidence on the thirteenth day of the trial. Reminding the jury of how Martin had been shot in the neck by police and had collapsed in a pool of blood when being arrested, he warned them that before they jumped to any conclusions or found themselves being affected by feelings of sympathy, they should also remember that when he was shot, Martin was in possession of two loaded handguns. He added that the disclosure of Martin's previous convictions could be 'a vital factor'. If a defendant attacked the integrity of prosecution witnesses, as Martin had done, said the judge, previous convictions could be referred to during the trial. He told the jury not to underestimate the seriousness of Martin's allegations – he was accusing police officers of inventing their story of how he drew a gun and as a result was shot. 'Such information, elicited in cross-examination may be of vital importance when you hear the police being accused of scandalous and wicked conduct,' said the judge, 'to know the sort of person it is, who is making the allegations.'

After deliberating for three hours on 10 October, the jury foreman told the judge that 'there was no prospect of reaching an agreement on all the counts' that day. Telling them, 'You must not be under any pressure; take as long as you like,' Mr Justice Kilner-Brown directed that the jury be sent to what the press referred to as 'a secret London hotel' for the night. He had previously revealed an almost avuncular side of his nature, praising the jury when they asked a question: 'May I say how very much I appreciate the fact that you are paying attention to the evidence?' and also showing concern for their catering arrangements: 'You must say if you are tea or coffee people.'

On 11 October, the jury returned their verdicts: guilty (by a majority of 11–1) of causing grievous bodily harm to PC Carr, with intent to resist arrest. He was also convicted of possessing the guns with intent to resist arrest when he was shot in the neck six weeks later. He was found guilty of breaking into the offices of *Guns Review* – which he admitted during his trial – and also the theft of the money from the robbery where the guard was shot. He might have known that there was going to be a snatch of the money, Martin had told the jury, but he had no idea that guns were going to be taken along, let alone used and he claimed he had not shot the security guard, it was the other man whose name he didn't know who had been responsible for that. Since the statement of the security guard had been read to the court, he was unable to be cross-examined, so Martin was acquitted of causing grievous bodily harm to the guard as well.

It seems slightly incredible that he was acquitted of the burglary at the gunsmiths in Covent Garden or the burglary at Eurotell Security Specialists where the surveillance equipment was stolen. He admitted being in possession of equipment stolen from Eurotell but that was not the same as being a burglar, who in that case had inelegantly sawn through the shop's grill to effect entry. He, Martin grandly told the jury, always used duplicate keys.

He was also acquitted of the thefts of the Volkswagen Golf convertible and the Mercedes and also the alternative charges of receiving them; it was quite possible, he had told the jury, that he might have borrowed these vehicles from a friend who had naturally neglected to tell him the cars were stolen. It is more understandable that he was also acquitted of possessing firearms with intent to endanger life, since the prosecution had dropped the charge of attempting to murder PC Carr. As Sir Ivan Lawrence later said, 'Seldom can a defendant have been given so many benefits of the doubt,' which I suppose is one way of describing those verdicts.

When it came to sentencing, Martin tried for the last time to assert his own form of authority on the court, by standing up and attempting to walk down to the cells before the judge could speak, but the security guards, who after fifteen days were quite possibly tired of Martin's behaviour, were having none of it. He was grabbed and pulled back, to hear Mr Justice Kilner-Brown say:

> The fact remains that the growing rise in the carrying of loaded
> guns has reached alarming proportions. Those who carry loaded
> guns to shoot their way out of impending arrest must accept very
> severe sentences, indeed. And that is what you are going to get. In my
> judgement, the least sentence I can impose is one of twenty-five years.

Martin 'appeared distressed by the sentence' and his latest
paramour, Natasha, who must have possessed limitless amounts of
patience vowed that she would 'wait for him'. The press, eager for
a predictably imbecile comment from Martin's father, got one: 'If
I had a gun, I'd go and shoot the judge, myself.'

In mitigation, Ivan Lawrence had stated, 'He is clearly a bad
man but by no means completely evil.' PC Carr's view of Martin
certainly took a different view, but he contented himself by
saying that he was 'just another nonentity'; and being described
as 'a nobody' was probably the unkindest cut that Martin could
have received. He had had his day in court. Martin was all set to
be consigned to the history books. It was all over – almost, but
not quite.

The Further Trials

The nine-month wait between arrest and trial was undoubtedly the longest in Finch and Jardine's lives. They had been committed to stand their trial at the Old Bailey from Horseferry Road Magistrates' Court by Magistrate Kenneth Harington on 17 March 1983.

Jardine had been born in 1945 and joined the Metropolitan Police twenty years later. He was posted to Acton on 'X' Division in West London and a year after joining there had been an explosion at an electrical substation and Jardine had crawled through the twisted wreckage to pull a workman, overcome by carbon dioxide fumes, to safety. In recognition of his bravery, he was awarded a testimonial from the Royal Humane Society. He later passed the advanced driving course at Hendon and became an area car driver and in June 1969, Jardine attended a basic firearms course where he qualified as a marksman. In the late 1970s, he became a member of the 'X' Division Crime Squad and in 1982 was selected for the C11 surveillance team.

Peter Finch had also been born in 1945 but had joined the police slightly earlier than Jardine. He had been commended on two occasions and had attended the basic firearms course in October 1981 and he too had qualified as a marksman; and to qualify for that classification, it meant that the officer had to have an aggregate score of 90 per cent or higher.

Speaking to me thirty years later, Jardine told me that during that long wait he had received the most enormous encouragement from his colleagues (even though he was kept segregated from them), as well as hundreds of letters of support, including one from the comedian Eric Sykes. 'The biggest problem I had was with the press,' he told me, 'especially the *News of the World*. They'd come right up to our house and photograph me through the window.' Matters became so bad with the intrusion of certain members of the press that when Jardine, his wife and two sons wanted to leave their house in Pinner, Middlesex, they would have to exit through the back door, go down the garden, then cross into a neighbour's garden to get to the family car which was parked streets away.

'I'm certain – in fact, I know – that my phone calls were intercepted,' Jardine told me and when I expressed surprise at why anyone from his own department (since C11 was responsible for telephone intercepts) would wish to do so, he shook his head. 'Not the police – the press,' he replied and on this matter he was absolutely adamant. However, many police officers in a similar dilemma have firmly believed that their telephone calls were intercepted by the press, but certainly not in this pre-2000, pre-digital case.

Peter Finch suffered similarly. 'I always had trouble with the press ever since my address appeared in the newspaper,' he told me. 'I used to exit and enter my house very quickly and I managed to ward off photographers until the Sunday before my trial when in the afternoon, I went with my two sons to a park behind my house. That Monday, on the front of the *Daily Mirror*, my photo with one of my sons appeared. Sods!'

Like Jardine, Finch received 'excellent treatment from my colleagues; they even had a whip-round which they sent me, every week'. Fellow police officer who were close friends were obliged to submit written requests to their senior officers to permit them to visit him in order not to fall foul of the Discipline Code. Finch too received much support, including from luminaries such as Sir John Mills and David Tomlinson.

Detective Inspector Bob Cook recalled driving along the A406 North Circular Road and seeing on a bridge, spanning the carriageway, painted in large white letters, 'Finch and Jardine – Guilty'. He believed it was there for months, although Jardine who also saw it thought it was there for years. 'I remember the 'J' of 'Jardine' was painted the wrong way round,' he told me, adding humorously, 'but it must be difficult to get something like that right, when you're painting upside down!'

At long last the trial of the two detectives commenced in No. 1 Court at the Old Bailey on 12 October 1983.

The judge was 68-year-old Mr Justice Sir David Croom-Johnson. The Second World War had interrupted his legal career and at the conclusion of hostilities, Sir David was discharged from the Royal Navy with the rank of Lieutenant Commander and for his highly dangerous work during the D-Day landings he was awarded the Distinguished Service Cross. He was much admired as a courteous, deep-thinking judge and a good listener, although as one of the Greenham Common women later opined, 'It would take a bomb to move him.'

Jardine had the immense good fortune to be defended by John Mathew QC who, according to *The Guardian*, 'looked like a bishop' but was an extremely sharp defence barrister. He, together with Finch's barrister, Michael Corkery QC, who had been appointed senior treasury counsel in 1970, had both prosecuted the organised gangs who had been targeted by the Yard's Serious Crime Squad.

In opposition, there were political and legal heavyweights. The prosecution was led by the current attorney-general. Robert Michael Oldfield Havers PC, QC (later Baron Havers), was known as Sir Michael Havers; his career was dogged with controversy. He had prosecuted in two of the most notable and long-running miscarriages of justice in English legal history – the Guilford Four and the Maguire Seven – which would later result in severe condemnation for him. In 1981, Sir Michael appeared for the prosecution in the case of Peter Sutcliffe ('The Yorkshire Ripper') who was charged with thirteen counts of murder. When Sutcliffe offered a plea to manslaughter on the grounds of diminished responsibility, this was accepted by Sir Michael but in an almost unheard of intervention, the trial judge demanded a detailed explanation of Sir Michael's reasoning for accepting the lesser plea and having heard it, overruled him – after a two-week trial, Sutcliffe was convicted of the murders. So the verdict was a triumph for Sir Michael – albeit one which had been forced upon him – but he let himself down badly when in his opening speech he mentioned Sutcliffe's victims, telling the jury, 'Some were prostitutes but perhaps the saddest part of the case is that some were not. The last six attacks were on totally respectable women.' Unsurprisingly, the English Collective of Prostitutes was incandescent with rage, accusing him of 'condoning the murder of prostitutes' and demonstrating outside the Old Bailey with placards. Fortunately, Sir Michael had Roy Amlot QC, a highly respected barrister who was then senior prosecuting counsel for the Crown and Mr E.J. Bevan QC to assist him.

Both defendants were charged with attempting to murder Steven Waldorf, both with causing him grievous bodily harm and for Finch, a further charge of inflicting grievous bodily harm;

this latter charge referred to the pistol-whipping. Each of these charges carried a maximum sentence of life imprisonment and to all these charges, they pleaded not guilty.

In fact, there was very little in the facts to dispute; the defendants naturally did not deny shooting Waldorf and the prosecution conceded that everything that happened was as the result of a genuine mistake by the officers; the question for the jury was: were their actions justified?

Not, of course, according to the attorney-general. 'It does not matter, in fact, whether it had been Waldorf or Martin because there was no need, in the submission of the Crown, to take those actions at that stage – either to shoot at him, as Jardine did when he was half-in, half-out of the car, or to fracture his skull with a revolver, as Finch did. Whether Finch was standing or crouching, in order to strike Waldorf hard, at least twice, surely he must have been in a position to stop him getting a gun, even if he had a gun to go for. If you are pistol-whipping a man that closely, you must be in a position to restrain him.'

Sir Michael added that there was 'a remarkable similarity between Waldorf and Martin,' adding, 'This is one of the misfortunes of the case you are now trying. In fact, Waldorf did not know Martin and had never met him.'

In addition, Sir Michael told the jury, 'He [Finch] then fired two shots into the rear nearside tyre, deflating it. Why that was necessary is difficult to see. The car was stuck in the traffic.' It appears that Sir Michael completely missed the point that in situations such as this was perceived to be, desperate men take desperate actions. Simply because a car is stuck in traffic, it does not mean that there is no way out; a car can mount the pavement or – in this case – could pull out to the offside, because there were no vehicles in the middle lane. Unlike police officers, desperate men do not have to observe the niceties of the Road

Traffic Act; they can and will drive incredibly recklessly to the danger of pedestrians and other road users, as Martin had already demonstrated. Of course, Purdy was driving and he could not remotely be described as being 'desperate' but Finch was not to know this and he had to make a split-second decision and he took it.

Students attending a firearms course are not told *not* to fire at tyres but as Acting Chief Superintendent Robert Wells stated, 'Students are merely told that the action is usually ineffective and dangerous.' Although television programmes and films depict tyres being deflated by means of gunshots, a fully inflated tyre is unlikely to be hit successfully to cause deflation and even a stationary tyre will resist most bullets fired by handguns. In fact, this stationary tyre *was* deflated by Finch firing at it; was this a correct course of action to take? With hindsight, it probably was.

Waldorf cut an impressive figure in court; pale and thin, with a voice that was sometimes barely audible, he nevertheless told the jury that he remembered 'vividly' much of what had happened that evening at Pembroke Road. When the shooting began, he initially thought it was between two other parties and that he had just been caught in the cross-fire, but soon 'It became pretty apparent I was the target. I was trying to think if I had any enemies. The car windows came in and the bullets kept coming through.'

Susan Stephens told the jury, 'Everything went white as the window shattered ... then there was a split second and I remember hearing shots and thinking it was terrorists.'[1]

Giving evidence, George Ness was asked what the police should have done and he replied, 'They should have made it

---

1. In fact, this was quite understandable; at that time, London was in the grip of a major IRA offensive.

clear they were armed police.' Asked whether Finch should have pistol-whipped Waldorf, Ness replied, 'I do not know. You cannot make an assessment in cold, clinical terms. The adrenaline and blood were flowing that night. He was facing a man he thought was dangerous.'

He went on to say that Finch had gone against standing orders by drawing his gun and firing into the tyre; he should, he told the attorney-general, have called out, 'Armed police.' He went on to say that if there had been any evidence of anyone in the car being armed, he should have told them to stay where they were.

However, Michael Corkery read out the official instructions for what armed police were to say when dealing with a car containing armed suspects:

> We are armed police. Driver, stop your engine, throw the keys out driver, open your door, put your feet on the road, put your hands on top of the open door and get out of the vehicle, slowly, turn and face me. Keep your arms outstretched. Now walk towards me, slowly. Stop. Get on your knees and lie down.

'Any officer dealing with Martin might well be dead before he got very far with that rigmarole,' observed Corkery and Ness agreed that that was possible. He also agreed that Finch was probably under considerable pressure, strain and stress and feared what might occur, but told the court 'What I would expect him to do is put himself in the position of whether it was Martin in the car, without putting himself in jeopardy and then come back to tell me.'

Jardine and Finch both gave evidence, reiterating their previous statements to the officers from CIB2 and Jardine told the jury, 'It would have been extremely foolish to have covered the man with a gun and then attempted to overpower and arrest him.' If it had been Martin, it would have been a contest to see who got shot first and Jardine added, 'I'm very much afraid I would have to act the same way again.'

Half way through the trial, the attempted murder charge against Finch was dropped and in summing up, the judge told the jury: 'I cannot emphasise too strongly there is one attitude you must not have in this case. That because an innocent man is shot, someone must have committed an offence of some sort. That is not so. Let me tell you what you are trying and what you are not trying.'

The judge said the jury were not trying the issue of whether or not the police should be armed or whether the general policing of law enforcement and law and order were being satisfactorily dealt with, nor were they trying the issue of whether the wrong man had been shot and somebody should pay. The intentions and state of mind of the two detectives were something which had to be taken into account and that could be difficult. The officers were entitled to fire first if it was done in 'an honest, genuine and reasonable' frame of mind. A 'pre-emptive strike' was justified in the right circumstances. He told the jury that if they were anything less than sure that the prosecution had proved its case, then the detectives were entitled to be acquitted. 'You must look at the situation as it was at the time, and as it presented itself to the two defendants,' he said.

'I'd been nervous all the way through the trial,' Jardine told me, 'but as I climbed the stairs from the cells for the verdict, I felt completely calm.' It was Wednesday 19 October and the jury of eight women and four men had retired for 105 minutes before unanimously finding both detectives not guilty of all the charges. As they were about to leave the court in separate taxis, an unnamed detective sergeant patted Finch on the back, saying, 'That's the right verdict. They were only doing their duty. No officer wants to cause anyone any great harm but it can become necessary when your life is in danger. If you are left with the split-second decision – if you don't fire, you are dead; if you do, you end up in the dock at the Old Bailey.' He continued, 'I'm sure both officers have the support of the general public who understand the situation they were in. Mr Finch is a quiet, honest, hard-working officer … a happy family man. There is no way he would have been considering revenge. That would be the very opposite of his nature.'

Opinions following the verdicts were understandably mixed. The Metropolitan Police were delighted with the result, although Assistant Commissioner Geoffrey Dear QPM, DL (later Baron Dear), who had the responsibility for firearms training, added a caveat: 'We regret the incident. I would like to say it will never happen again. It would be impossible for anyone to say that, but we will do our very best.' The chairman of the then 120,000-strong Police Federation, Leslie Curtis, added a cautionary note when he addressed a federation meeting at Southampton: 'If the only rule that applies to an armed police officer is going to be "You are on your own and God help you if you make a mistake," then we have a problem.'

Over thirty years after the event, Neil Dickens told me, 'In this unfortunate particular event, both the Waldorf family and the police officers and their families were all victims; they all gave their full support to the investigation.' Labour MP Robert Kilroy-Silk, a spokesman on home affairs, said, 'What I am very worried about is to ensure that we eradicate any semblance of a "Starsky and Hutch"[2] mentality that might exist in the police. I am going to raise the matter with the Home Secretary.' The

---

2. A popular and gung-ho, gun-toting American police detective TV series of that time.

National Council for Civil Liberties told the Home Secretary precisely how his duties should be discharged, adding, 'The public can have no confidence that this appalling incident will not be repeated.' These were sentiments echoed by the left-wing press who, a week after the acquittal, roared their displeasure. Telling their readers that they were 'startled' by the verdict, they asked for the retired judge from the Court of Appeal Lord Denning's views on the verdict. Unfortunately, this rather backfired on them after he opined 'the verdict was absolutely right'. 'So be it. As he says, the jury is the jury. We might add, the judge is the judge,' the readers were told, adding nastily and perhaps even libellously, 'Mr Justice Croom-Johnson got the result he wanted.'

But apart from wanting Finch and Jardine hung, drawn and quartered, the newspaper thundered:

> Blame for what happened rests not only with the men who pulled the trigger but with those who sent them out incautiously prepared and wrongly briefed. The whole operation was badly controlled, with an all-but-fatal ending. To those who call this a counsel of perfection one must reply that the British public is entitled to expect the highest degree of care when policemen carry firearms. The senior officers, as well as those acquitted in court, should now face a disciplinary hearing. Otherwise, the commissioner's – and the home secretary's – reassurances will not be convincing.

Probably the most dignified response came from Steven Waldorf's mother, Beryl. She and her husband Len had kept a vigil at the hospital as their son fought for his life. Now she said, 'We are not vindictive. As long as Steven is all right, that is all that matters. We feel pleased for the detectives and their families because they must have been living a nightmare.' In the circumstances, it was an exceedingly generous observation.

As for Steven Waldorf, he stated that he was not surprised at the verdict, adding, 'I don't think I could ever forgive them but I can't blame them. It's the system that's at fault, not them. When you think that they fired fourteen shots and only five hit me – and none of them killed me – that had to be luck. It was lucky for me the police were bad shots. At least, I think it was luck. I don't know whether we're lucky or unlucky when the police are incompetent.'

The Police Federation was furious when on 14 December 1983 Thames Television televised an edition of *TV Eye* which depicted a dramatisation of the shooting in Pembroke Road. Actor John Arthur (who had played the part of police officers on several occasions) took the role of DC Peter Finch and Jonathan Morris played the part of Steven Waldorf, to whom, not unnaturally, he bore more than a passing resemblance. Waldorf assisted in reconstructing details of the incident, saying, 'It was a very fair portrayal. It was an interesting experience watching the reconstruction. I helped make the programme because I thought it was something I needed to get out of my system, and it did.'

The reason for the Federation's fury was because no decision had yet been reached regarding the ultimate fate, under the disciplinary code, in respect of detective constables Finch and Jardine and claimed that the programme had increased pressure to have charges brought which, if they were found guilty, could result in dismissal, forced resignation, demotion or a fine. 'ITV is seeking to conduct a trial by television of a case which has already been decided by a judge and jury,' snapped Tony Judge, a Federation spokesman. 'If disciplinary charges are brought against these officers there will be no precedent for the climate of prejudice that will surround their case. This programme, with its lurid enactment of the shooting incident can only put extra pressure on the two constables and upon the senior officers at Scotland Yard who may yet have to sit in judgement upon them. The Federation is very angry about this programme.'

However, the Independent Police Complaints Board, chaired by Sir Cyril Philips (who had already headed a Royal Commission into criminal procedure during 1978 to 1981), sat just prior to Christmas 1983 and the findings of the board matched those suggestions made by Deputy Assistant Commissioner James Sewell QPM, the head of the Yard's Complaints Investigation Bureau, following a detailed special investigation. Sewell's recommendations were endorsed and approved by the deputy commissioner, Albert Laugharne CBE, QPM, and it was decided that no disciplinary proceedings against any of the officers would be instituted and the officers were reinstated. However, their authority to carry firearms was withdrawn and it was made clear that 'they will not be called on to use firearms again in their service'.

Finch told me he saw Ness once at court 'and then at home after the trial, saying I couldn't return as a CID officer. I can understand not being a firearms officer but return to uniform? What's the difference? I would still be in contact with the public.' He was returned to uniform duties at Ruislip police station. He was asked to help setting up the Neighbourhood Watch scheme and then took over the crime prevention officer's job. It was the type of employment that suited Finch, but as new senior management came to the station who were unaware of his circumstances he was sent on Central London demonstrations and his health suffered; he was medically discharged from the force in 1991.

Jardine resumed duties with the C11 surveillance team until 1988, when he took up duties with the No. 2 Area Force Intelligence Bureau. He retired in December 1995 and moved out of the London area.

On 14 November 1983, the trial of Stephens, Purdy and Enter commenced at Knightsbridge Crown Court, before His Honour Judge Anthony Babington. To many defendants the judge must have appeared to have been an 'amiable old buffer' speaking in plummy tones with a marked stutter; he was, in fact, a remarkable man. During the Second World War, he had a passionate affair with a beautiful 19-year-old WREN. He sustained a terrible head injury following the fighting with the Royal Ulster Rifles around Arnhem and was returned home paralysed down his right side and mute (the speech-related part of his brain had been destroyed) and she refused to see him again. He regained his speech by utilising another part of his brain, learned to write with his left hand, was called to the Bar, and became a prosecuting counsel, a Metropolitan Stipendiary Magistrate and now a formidable circuit judge.

The prosecution was led by Barbara Mills QC (later Dame Barbara and also the Director of Public Prosecutions), an extremely astute barrister. Stephens was charged with four counts of handling goods stolen by Martin, and Purdy and Enter, two similar charges; all the defendants pleaded not guilty.

Briefly, the facts of the case were that Stephens had put the property into storage at Pickfords on 16 August 1982, using the name she had used as a model and had paid the majority of the storage charges. However, payment of the charges fell into arrears and near to Christmas 1982, Pickfords sent her a final reminder. She telephoned the company, telling them that she had had an accident and that she would settle the account after Christmas. There the property had remained until two weeks after Martin's escape from Marlborough Street Magistrates' Court when she, Purdy and Enter had collected it and taken it to Enter's flat at Ladbroke Grove where it was discovered when he was arrested. In fact, said Mrs Mills, it was alleged by the Crown that Steven Waldorf had been present when the property had been moved.

Because of the sheer quantity of the property, two trips had to be made on consecutive days, 6 and 7 January 1983. Stephens had paid the outstanding amount of £74 and Purdy signed for the goods using the name 'Perry' – this, in fact, was his mother's maiden name.

On the second occasion, it was alleged that only Stephens and Purdy were involved, taking the property to Enter's flat which was put into a spare bedroom. The three defendants all gave different stories when they were arrested, said Mrs Mills, plus by the time the police raided Enter's flat two weeks later, two of the chests containing the stolen goods had disappeared. Detective Sergeant Roger Driscoll told the court that when he had searched the Mini in Pembroke Road on the night of the shooting, he had found Purdy's wallet which contained the £74 storage receipt from Pickfords. I gave evidence that Enter had claimed that Stephens had told him that the containers held her clothes but he had looked and saw that the boxes contained 'Martin's stuff'. 'I don't know where it all came from,' he said, 'but I knew it was Martin's. I know he is a villain and I know it couldn't have been straight.'

Cross-examined by Richard Crabtree for the defence, I was accused of grabbing Enter by his shirt front, telling him, 'We're not the local nancy-pansy boys; we're the Flying Squad.' Naturally, the allegation was untrue and I denied it, but the 'nancy-pansy boys' jibe followed me around for years!

Stephens stated that she believed the items to be household goods and had no reason to believe they had been stolen and Purdy admitted that he was suspicious and thought that some of the property was stolen. In a statement made by him that I read out to the court, Purdy stated in part, 'It just didn't seem right that a girl should have that sort of stuff.'

Stephens admitted in court that it was her information which had helped police catch Martin but denied that she had accepted or had been offered a reward; in fact, on the few times she had met him between escape and capture, she had, she said, entreated Martin to give himself up. However, she told the jury that she was 'in no doubt' that after Martin's arrest in September 1983, she had told police of the whereabouts of the property at Pickfords, but they had never taken her up on it. Several officers were called in rebuttal to say that she had never mentioned the goods in storage, which made sound sense; had she informed the police, it was in their interests to recover the property as soon as possible, not months later.

Stephens said that after Martin's arrest, she had gone to see him at Brixton prison but that she became bored with having to visit him. 'He was obsessed with me all day and I was trying to drop him nicely,' she told the court. In addition, she said that Purdy had become her boyfriend – she had told police this when she was first interviewed following the shooting at Pembroke Road – but after pressure from Martin's probation officer and vicar, who told her he would go on hunger strike or commit suicide, she returned to see him at Brixton. 'Without that pressure,' she informed the jury, 'I would never have gone to see him again.'

On the fourth day of the trial, Stephens was cleared, on the directions of Judge Babington on one of the charges of receiving stolen goods, which included security equipment and surveillance devices. However, the second receiving charge was still in place, as were two more charges alleging handling the goods for David Martin's benefit. It appeared that little if any of the trio's testimony impressed the jury of seven women and five men who on 21 November found the three defendants guilty. Judge Babington told them:

> All three of you have been convicted on the clearest evidence of offences concerned with lending assistance to a very dangerous criminal by helping him to conceal proceeds of a crime.

Stephens, who had no previous convictions, had been represented by Ronald Thwaites QC, a barrister described as 'capable of producing results that others can only dream of', but not, alas, on this occasion. He told the court that she had helped the police catch Martin, stated that she had received several poison pen letters, that she would 'be in danger in jail' and that she now wanted to start a new life carrying out voluntary work in Africa. However, as the judge told Stephens, 'No doubt you were infatuated for a time by David Martin. That is a reason for your offence but not an excuse' and sentenced her to six months' imprisonment. Purdy, who had had several minor brushes with the law including a spell of Borstal Training, was sentenced to nine months' imprisonment, as was Enter; the following day, they sought leave to appeal against their sentences, which were duly suspended. This leniency was reflected in a comment by Steve Holloway: 'My view of these people was that they were not out-and-out criminals; but just people who got caught up in situations which happened to be criminal.'

The day before the trio were sentenced, there was a column in the *Sunday Express* which mentioned that the allegation had been made in court that Steven Waldorf had helped the defendants move Martin's stolen property. 'May we be told why Mr. Waldorf is not in the dock with them?' was the question posed by the newspaper. The answer is quite simple. The matter was referred to the Director of Public Prosecutions. Having carefully considered all the circumstances of the case, he decided – as he did in the case of Detective Constable John Deane – to take no further action.

The End of the Road

While he had been on remand at Brixton prison awaiting trial, Martin had begun a sentimental albeit unlikely friendship with the serial killer Dennis Nilsen. Prison officers saw them constantly whispering together and came to the conclusion that they were plotting an escape and separated them. Nilsen was apparently so upset that he attacked three warders with a chamber pot.[1]

However, following Martin's conviction, the couple were briefly reunited at Parkhurst maximum security prison. Nilsen had been convicted of six counts of murder and two of attempted murder and had been sentenced to life imprisonment, with a whole life tariff. Martin told his friend, 'Twenty-five years is worse than a life sentence. If I can't get out of here, I'll kill myself.' In fact, during their last meeting, Martin had told Mark Bryant, 'I won't do my time in prison.' Separated from 'Natasha' and now also Nilsen, Martin resumed his correspondence with Stephens. He had already told police, plus anybody else who would listen, if his demands were not met 'you will have a dead body on your hands'.

'I just want to see you once more and then I will end it. That is the escape' was part of one of the letters he had previously

---

1. This appeared to be a favoured weapon; already on 1 August 1983, he had thrown the contents of a chamber pot over several warders, thereby earning himself fifty-six days' solitary confinement.

written to Stephens from Brixton prison, and in another: 'You are the only one who can help me, as your love is all that can bring me my happiness or release me from the life I lead.' Stephens later said, 'I honestly think that he will do it. To cage him up for twenty-five years is to say that the man has no future. He is the kind of man who likes to be active. He is very intelligent and will go mad in jail. I fear for what is going to happen.' While on remand at Brixton, Martin had been taken to hospital having swallowed a cocktail of paracetamol and barbiturates.

Among Martin's fellow prisoners at Parkhurst were Donald Neilson, the so-called 'Black Panther' who in 1976 had been convicted of a series of armed robberies and murders, the fourth of whom was Lesley Whittle, an heiress, and Neilson had been sentenced to life imprisonment, with a whole life tariff; and Henry MacKenny, who had been convicted of four contract murders in 1980 and who would be cleared on appeal twenty-three years later. Martin's mind was now unravelling. He had been noted as a potential suicide risk and had been placed in a special security wing at Parkhurst with six or seven other prisoners where there was a high staff ratio. He had become involved in a row with Neilson regarding the use of a video recorder which Martin used a lot; on this occasion, he wanted to record a nature programme but it was Neilson's turn to use it. When Senior Prison Officer Donald Smith ordered Martin back to his cell, he became 'very hysterical' and as Smith would tell the inquest held on 21 May 1984 at Newport, Isle of Wight, 'He had lost face with the other prisoners. The other prisoners knew he was in the wrong. One of them had told him, "Come on, David, go back to your cell and grow up."'

Martin was put on a special fifteen-minute observation, later lifted to a thirty-minute watch. The following day, Smith tried to persuade him to get back into normal prison routine because when he got into a black mood, he would generally emerge from his cell, to associate with Neilson or MacKenny and he would then have a cup of coffee with them.

But not this time. Martin was found hanged in his cell on 13 March 1984; in a bizarre twist, it was the same cell that Terrance John Clark aka Terry Sinclair, jailed for a gangland murder, had been found dead, ostensibly from a heart attack, the previous year. Prison Officer Jonathan Austin had visited Martin's cell that evening to find the door ajar and the light turned off. 'I pushed the door three or four inches and I could feel something behind it,' he told the inquest jury. 'It turned out to be a chair. As I entered the cell, on the right, I could see Martin hanging with flex around his neck.' Martin had used a piece of flex, taken from a prison washing machine. The plug was then re-fitted on the remaining cable so that no one would know that the twenty-one inch length of flex was missing. Even in death, Martin was meticulous in his preparations; and for the last time in his life, he was, as always, in complete control. A note to Susan Stephens, found beside his body contained the passages: 'All I have is death to take away the pain of not being with you ... Whatever death is, it can't be as bad as waiting each day to see you – and not.'

The principal medical officer at Parkhurst said that Martin's paramount problem was his obsession about getting back together with Stephens who had not visited him since beginning his sentence. Senior Prison Officer Smith concurred, saying, 'I think this time, David Martin had decided to kill himself and he was trying to draw attention to this fact because normally he would not argue over the video.' Psychiatrist Dr Brian Cooper had examined Martin on several occasions. He told the inquest, 'Martin was a clever and resourceful man and there is some doubt as to whether this was a genuine suicide attempt. He came from a group of people in prison who put very little value on their lives and who try to use them as blackmail.' Cross-examined by James

Storman, solicitor for the Martin family, Dr Cooper was asked if he believed Martin would try to kill himself if his relationship with Sue Stephens totally ended; his reply was 'Yes.' 'Do you think he ever got over Sue Stephens?' asked Storman and the psychiatrist answered, 'No.'

The jury, having also heard from Ralph, Martin's father, returned a verdict of suicide. Upon hearing the news, Steven Waldorf's father said, 'I never met David Martin,' and then characteristically added, 'but I am rather sad to hear that he is dead.'

In interviews with the press, Martin Sr was almost triumphant about his son's demise, while taking the opportunity to blame everybody else for it. He told *Daily Mail* reporters, with the type of rhetoric which had become his trademark:

> When they gave him twenty-five years, they might as well have put a bullet through his head. I knew weeks ago that this would happen. He told me. He said there was no way he could do all that time. The governor of the prison wrote to me saying maybe he would settle down and do his time. But he was thirty-seven – how can you face twenty-five years in prison at thirty-seven?
>
> He has taken the can back for the Waldorf shooting. To me, he has done them in the eye. He is better off where he is now. It is the police and the system that killed him. I told them all what would happen and they did nothing. David was cleverer than any of them. He just bided his time until he got the opportunity. Nobody can hurt him anymore. In the finish, he beat them anyway.

I suppose it's difficult to argue against logic that is as twisted as that.

Steven Waldorf recovered from his gunshot wounds and sued the police, who did not fight the case. He was reputedly awarded £120,000 – and that wasn't all. Following his retirement, Commander Frank Cater wrote his memoirs entitled *The Sharp End*. In it, there was an account of the Martin case, which contained the words '… the injured man was in fact, not David Martin – he was a friend of Martin's, Steven Waldorf'. Of course, this was untrue; in fact, everyone had been at pains to say that the two had never met and once more, Waldorf sued, this time for libel against Cater and his publishers, The Bodley Head. Cater and his co-author Tom Tullett agreed there was no truth in the suggestion, saying that the libellous piece had been added during the editing, after the authors had delivered the manuscript to the publishers, but the fact remained it had appeared in published form. On 19 January 1990, Waldorf's barrister Geoffrey Shaw told the High Court before Mr Justice Popplewell, 'The effect of that wrong statement, in its context, was to convey the suggestion that Mr Waldorf had been assisting Martin to avoid arrest' and Waldorf received substantial damages plus costs.

Susan Stephens too had taken legal action. A writ dated 23 April 1985 was served on the commissioner, Jardine and Finch, demanding 'exemplary damages' stating that she was an innocent bystander in 'a reckless, precipitous and random ambush' and as a result of the bullet wound to her back had been obliged to stop her lucrative career as a model. This action, like the others, was not defended and Stephens received substantial damages, reportedly £10,000. Coincidentally, that was the amount awarded to PC Carr by the Criminal Injuries Compensation Board for being shot in the groin – and almost losing his life – by Martin.

The BBC *Panorama* programme with the title 'Lethal Force' was televised on 9 December 2001, featuring the presenter Tom Mangold and Steven Waldorf. *Open Fire*, a 1994 made-for-television film directed by Paul Greengrass, depicted the case where David Martin was played by Rupert Graves, whose performance was very compelling. Susan Stephens and Don Brown both assisted in the film's making.

The police kept hold of the yellow Mini for far too long; the Portobello Car Hire Company successfully sued the police for thousands of pounds worth of loss of rental, far more than the car was worth. It led to a change of policy; nowadays in the event of a similar unhappy incident, the police purchase the vehicle immediately.

So what happened next?

There was such a public outcry following Waldorf's shooting that the government knew that something decisive had to be done with regards to police firearms training and on 22 March 1983, it was. It might be thought that action taken almost two months after that near-fatal shooting was not particularly fast, especially when compared to the split-second decisions which had to be made by armed police officers, but by governmental standards this response was akin to greased lightning.

A Home Office circular 47/1983 was sent to every chief constable in England and Wales, together with new 'Guidelines on the Issue and Use of Firearms by Police' and in addition those chief officers were informed that in the next few days, copies of this circular would arrive in the libraries of both Houses of Parliament. It was a clever bit of back-covering by the Home Office. By taking this course of action, the message conveyed was that these guidelines were not negotiable, they were in the public domain and whatever instructions those forces had observed before they had better change to this new national version immediately. And if anyone did not, they would be on their own; it would certainly not be the fault of the Home Office.

Therefore, from now on the issue of firearms had to be authorised by an officer of Association of Chief Police Officers (ACPO) rank, commander in the Metropolitan Police, assistant chief constable in provincial forces. If a delay might result in loss of life or serious injury, the authorisation could be granted by an officer of superintendent or chief superintendent rank, although in that eventuality, a senior officer of ACPO rank had to be informed as soon as possible and then any authority which had been granted could be rescinded, if, for example, the threat level had diminished or through the ACPO officer's general unwillingness. The exception was that a standing authority was given for those officers on protection duty, those who were responsible for the safety and well-being of politicians, including the Home Secretary.

For the Home Office, who with a large sigh of relief had metaphorically passed the queen of spades, the next step was to appoint a national working party and this was discussed at the ACPO Joint Steering Committee on 5 May 1983. Geoffrey Dear, Assistant Commissioner 'D' Department, was asked to chair the party and their brief was 'to examine and recommend means of improving the selection and training of police officers as authorised firearms officers, with particular reference to temperament and stress'. The Dear Report was published that November and its recommendations stated that all officers selected for training should undergo psychological written tests, the duration of the basic course should be extended to ten days and that refresher training should be increased to four times per year on two consecutive days.

The Metropolitan Police policy committee sat in May 1984 and the recommendations of the Dear Report were split into two; the first phase agreed the psychological testing, the increase of the basic course plus one extra refresher day, although there could be no increase in the budget. A decision on phase two, including additional staff and facilities, was deferred until December. It was estimated that a budget of between £3 and 10 million would be needed; however, a few days later it was decided that the majority of the funds would be allocated to the building of police stations and a miniscule amount would go to 'phase two'. In 1985, a mock-up 'street' was constructed at Lippitts Hill training centre by the instructors themselves. Some single-storey plywood building facades were added in 1993, scarcely an improvement. The following year, nearby residents complained about the levels of noise generated by the camp and so training was restricted and in 2003, it closed and a new training area was opened.

Since the time of the Waldorf shooting and up to 2014, Metropolitan Police officers have shot dead twenty-two people. Some, like the case of Jean Charles de Menezes, unarmed and again 'the wrong man', were heartbreakingly tragic. The majority of the other shootings were fully justified although warranted or not, the outcome has usually been differing degrees of civil disobedience. So has the police perception of wishing to be armed changed since 1883 when 70 per cent of the officers polled wanted just that? Indeed it has; in a 2006 poll, 43 per cent of the respondents wanted an increase of authorised firearms officers. However, an overwhelming 82 per cent declined to be routinely armed.

I thought that the Martin case had been a perfect example of how a dedicated team of detectives could be plucked out of their normal duties and channelled into a top-level investigation. It happened later in the year when that same team of officers supplemented the Flying Squad's Walthamstow office when they investigated the Security Express robbery at Shoreditch in which underworld luminaries such as Ronnie Knight and the Kray's henchman, Freddie Forman, would figure so prominently. It happened again that year when gold bullion valued at £26 million was stolen from the Brink's-Mat warehouse near Heathrow.

Citing these two cases, it seemed to me that inescapable logic demanded the Flying Squad should keep a central reserve. To my great dismay, within a short period of time, the remainder of the squads at the Yard were devolved and assimilated into the area offices.

Cater retired from the force in January 1985 and Don Brown, a month later. I always thought that he, plus Nicky Benwell, Davy Walker and the others who dashed into that pitch-black tunnel in pursuit of Martin, would receive gallantry awards. But they received nothing, no gongs, no commendations, no 'well dones.' It was thought politically incorrect to praise the men who had caught Martin because of the stigma attached to the case, where an innocent man had been shot by police who were not connected in any way with the Flying Squad. It was the type of gutlessness which should have caused the mandarins at both Scotland Yard and Whitehall to hang their heads in shame.

I know that Peter Finch was also being considered for a bravery award for the arrest of Martin at Crawford Place; with the shooting of Waldorf, that went *straight* out of the window. The only semblance of recognition went to PC Carr. For wrestling with Martin to try to take the gun off him and incidentally getting shot in the process, he was awarded a Deputy Assistant

Commissioner's Commendation. It was the lowest award the Metropolitan Police could bestow, and in PC Carr's case, it was an insult.

After his release from hospital, Carr was off sick for six months. He then resumed duty at Marylebone Lane but in 1985, while carrying out an arrest, he chipped his elbow and was taken off frontline duties to work in the Criminal Prosecutions Office. He then raised and ran the charge centre at Wembley Stadium until 1995 when he worked at Harrow police station. Ten years later, he retired, having served thirty years. From time to time, he still experiences discomfort from the effects of the gunshot.

George Ness was later promoted to the rank of commander, was appointed the head of the Flying Squad, awarded the Queen's Police Medal for distinguished service and retired in 1993.

Neil Dickens and Michael Taylor were both promoted to the rank of deputy assistant commissioner, were similarly awarded the Queen's Police Medal and retired, respectively, in 1994 and 1995.

Lester Purdy told me that he and Marion Waldorf had been drifting apart but the shooting brought them back together and they married in 1985. However, he experienced trauma; as he told me, 'I had a lot of hang-ups regarding Steve getting shot and dealing with the fact that I ran and left him and Sue,' and a psychiatrist suggested that he was suffering from post-traumatic stress disorder. For a variety of reasons, he and Marion later divorced. Purdy was employed project managing communication installations and in 1987, met his future second wife. They and their family now live in the South of England.

Steven Waldorf, Purdy tells me, is believed to be doing well in the property business in North London. Peter Enter moved to the North of England for many years but he and Purdy met up again in 2002 when Purdy employed him for a short while, using

Enter's electrician's expertise to install mainframe computers; they lost touch in 2004 when Purdy moved.

As for Sue Stephens, Purdy said, 'After the shooting, she went back to her mum's. She had health problems and I know the whole thing affected her greatly. She told me she had met a guy in Topsham.' In 2000, Stephens is believed to have moved to Europe.

One by one, several of my contemporaries on the case died; Nicky Benwell, who had been awarded a Queen's Police Medal for his sterling work in Northern Ireland, Tony Freeman, Graham Newell, Tony Brightwell, Cam Burnell, Davy Walker – and Don Brown. Don died in August 2007 from mesothelioma, a rare form of cancer almost always caused by exposure to asbestos dust; its development can take between ten and forty years to materialise. His widow Linda always believed that this had been caused by Don's exposure to the asbestos contained in tube train's brake linings from when he went down the tunnel after Martin. However, she also recalled that when he returned home after the incident, his suit was covered in white powder and it had to be taken to the dry cleaners. What she was not aware of was that in 1932, an experiment to soundproof a 430-yard stretch of the southbound Northern Line tunnel, between Golders Green and Hampstead stations, using blue asbestos had been carried out.

Since that time, Transport for London has attempted to rid the Underground system of asbestos while at the same time stating that its level in the atmosphere is far below danger level. At the time of writing, there is a new estimated date of 2017 for the tunnels to be cleaned, although Transport for London still asserts that the dust levels were 'highly unlikely' to cause serious damage to human health. The organisation Clean Air in London disagrees; and so does Linda Brown. Was that Don Brown's reward for his gallantry – a painful, lingering death, instead of the medal he so richly deserved?

Following the shooting of Waldorf and the final arrest of Martin, there was a great deal of speculation and rumour; and to a certain extent, in the immediate aftermath of the event, this was understandable. But as the years passed, when people really should have known better, the hearsay went viral and what was arrant nonsense became accepted as fact.

For example, it was said that the yellow Mini was not hired but stolen. One rumour had Waldorf driving and completely unaware that Susie Stephens had somehow crept into the back, unnoticed by him. Another was that Waldorf was in the back of the car, and Stephens in the front and also that there were two women in the back. One rumour which made its way into print was that after Finch had shot Waldorf, he aimed his empty gun between Waldorf's eyes, said, 'OK, cocksucker,' and pulled the trigger. It was alleged that both Martin and Waldorf had been shot by members of the Flying Squad and that months later, it was discovered that there were goods stolen by Martin in the Mini.

It was stated quite categorically that Martin had shot PC Carr *after* escaping from Great Marlborough Street Magistrates' Court on Christmas Eve. Also Martin was hanged *before* he could stand trial and during his escape into Hampstead Underground station, he had got into a train driver's cab, in possession of a sawn-off shotgun, telling the driver that he was a signals engineer and best of all, when he was pursued through the underground tunnel, he was in drag and was glad to be caught 'because these high heels are killing me'.

In addition, one of the strongest rumours put about by those of the criminal classes who have achieved a thin veneer of education and are actually able to put one consecutive word in front of another, was that a 'shoot on sight' policy existed in respect of Martin. Slightly more articulate sections of the left-wing press suggested that there were government sanctioned death squads. Neither was true and I hope that this book has gone a long way to disprove those assertions; to sensible readers, that is. Nothing that I or anybody else says will make one jot of difference to the unshakable faith that the criminals have in their accusations, but consider this: if such a policy existed, wouldn't it have made sense for the Flying Squad – whom the criminals detest more than any other branch of the Metropolitan Police – to have utilised that dictum in the Underground tunnel at Belsize Park and shot Martin dead? They didn't, because of course no such instruction existed.

It's easy, I know, to be wise after the event. Hindsight, that attribute with which all defence barristers are blessed, is a wonderful thing. But whenever the matter of the shooting of Steven Waldorf and the hunt for David Martin is mentioned, the question will inevitably arise: should Detective Constable Peter Finch have been instructed to have gone out alone on foot and armed to attempt to identify the man in the yellow Mini as being David Martin?

My opinion is 'No.' I give it because I spent much of my career being involved in confrontational and often dangerous situations. Sometimes I would have sufficient time to work out a plan, to evaluate the risks, minimise them as much as possible and balance my decision on the success or not of the mission; on other occasions, I had to trust my gut instinct and go in with my head down; and sometimes it worked and sometimes it didn't. But that was not the case on this occasion. The operation had been planned twenty-four hours in advance.

Look at the facts. On 15 September 1982, Finch confronted a highly dangerous criminal who, within the space of the previous six weeks, had shot and seriously wounded a security guard during a robbery and shortly thereafter, had also shot and again almost killed a fellow police officer. And yet, at the time of the confrontation, Finch was unaware that the person he was addressing was the wanted man; in fact, he believed him to be a woman. In the ensuing struggle, Martin had produced a fully loaded handgun and then, when he relinquished hold of it, when Finch thought the threat was over, he suddenly produced a second and fully loaded pistol and threatened him with that. Martin was shot at point-blank range by a colleague – and that shot was in a very close proximity to Finch as well. Splattered with Martin's blood, dazed and shocked by the whole incident, Finch was led away to the police station. It was an incident filled with trauma, from top to bottom.

Nowadays Finch would have rightly received counselling. In those days, due to the police force's macho image, the thought of seeing a psychiatrist would have been unthinkable. It was not until 13 October 1986 that the Police Welfare Service enlarged its scope to cover 'occupational problems' with a welfare officer on call, outside normal hours. In fact, psychiatric counselling was not routinely considered for undercover officers who often perform the most hazardous of operations for another ten years, whereas their Dutch and Belgian counterparts received it whether they wanted counselling or not. So it was only in 1990, when Finch was placed sick with stress, that it was suggested he seek psychiatric help.

Then just over three months later Martin escaped from court. Handguns from the gunsmiths burglary were still outstanding. No one was under any illusions as to how dangerously out of control and cunning Martin was, least of all Finch. And yet, two weeks later, after what appeared to be credible evidence having been received that Martin was going to reappear, Finch was once more armed and put into an OP in the expectation that he would be able to identify Martin. Should he have been on that operation at all? I think not.

The ideal person to be both in the OP and the operation would have been Detective Constable Fred Arnold. He had spent the most time with Martin. In fact, he was available; he and other officers were listening on the RT set in the incident room at Paddington Green, 'Delta 18', as the drama unfolded. That there should have been armed officers, quite separate from the C11 officers on that operation, I do not dispute. If the situation had arisen where it was absolutely necessary to arrest Martin on the street, independent authorised shots would be needed to effect that arrest, rather than to rely purely upon the clandestine role of the armed officers of C11.

And when it became clear that the person thought to be Martin had got into that yellow Mini, there was absolutely no necessity for anybody to reconnoitre on foot, especially not – had he been present – Fred Arnold, with his distinctive six foot five appearance, as well as being someone very well known to Martin. All that was needed would have been for Arnold to get into the C11 taxi. It could then have unobtrusively driven alongside the Mini, Arnold would have looked out from behind the taxi's darkened windows, and with the occupants of the Mini unable to see him, he could have carried out a safe identification of the man in the front passenger seat.

Perhaps Arnold might have made the same mistake as Finch over the identity of the Mini's passenger but if he had, what of it? The Mini would quite simply have been followed until its final destination and, had the passenger been Martin, he could have been safely housed until the reins were taken over by D11 operatives. On the other hand, if it had been established that the passenger in the Mini was not Martin, a decision would have been made, either to continue or abort the operation.

However, as I have already mentioned, in those days D11 were not involved in mobile plots, only static ones. So why not have involved the Flying Squad in the operation? One specialist unit, C11, had been called in from the Yard, so why not another? I do not pretend that the Flying Squad was the be-all and end-all in the police world, but undeniably that unit had the world's best drivers and over the squad's previous sixty years they had become experts at chasing, boxing in and if necessary ramming target vehicles. What was more, armed squad officers were renowned at carrying out what is now euphemistically known as 'hard stops'. The Flying Squad's presence was there for the asking.

I passed my opinion on Fred Arnold's suggested involvement to him and he agreed unequivocally with it. My opinion of whether or not Finch should have been there was a view shared by several people that I spoke to. Steve Holloway said, 'Peter Finch had been armed by the SIO [Senior Investigating Officer] – major mistake – the guy was probably still traumatised from his last encounter with Martin. No disrespect to Finch – he was put into a situation that he should not have been.'

In particular, I contacted a former member of the Metropolitan Police Firearms Unit, a National Firearms Instructor and Tactical Advisor. The author of *The Good Guys Wear Black*, who writes under the pen name 'Steve Collins', had this to say:

> I totally agree with you that Finch should never have been there, certainly in an armed capacity. I believe that given his history with

Martin he was probably suffering from Post Traumatic Stress Disorder (PTSD).[1] The very fact that he drew his firearm as he approached the vehicle leads me to suspect that he had already formed the opinion in his own mind that his nemesis Martin was going to be in the vehicle. From that moment on, everything went wrong and he simply shot in a panic to survive.

Let's take what went wrong:

- Finch approached the vehicle alone, weapon drawn.
- He opened fire on a vehicle full of occupants without considering his backdrop.
- He later goes on to pistol whip the suspect.
- Deane, on the other hand, opened fire on a vehicle full of people without identifying his target or knowing the full facts.

I can understand the actions of Jardine who believed it was Martin and he was reaching for a gun.

Personally, I feel sorry for the guy [Finch] who was obviously distraught and I feel angry at the senior officers that put him in that position after such a short time following the previous incident.

I believe that with the Intel they had, they should have continued the surveillance until the vehicle stopped at an address and the suspect identified … even if it was Martin in the vehicle, <u>nobody at that point was in danger</u>. [Author's underlining]

However, Peter Finch took a completely opposite view. 'Should I have been there?' he asked me rhetorically. 'I wouldn't have wanted it any other way. I arrested him and nearly lost my life. I

---

1. This condition can materialise in as little as one month after being involved in a traumatic incident.

wanted him behind bars again. I would have objected if I wasn't on the squad. Maybe other officers would have also ID'd Waldorf as Martin, because they were so much alike. Maybe it was a mistake others could have made.'

It's interesting to read Finch's comment 'I wanted him behind bars again' because there exists a parallel between what happened in Pembroke Road and when Woman Police Constable 325 'Z' Kathleen Flora Parrott acted as a decoy to try to catch a violent rapist in 1955. She was attacked and badly physically and sexually assaulted by the man, who escaped. But after five weeks off sick, she resumed the decoy patrol and the perpetrator, an ex-commando, was caught and convicted. Over half a century later, when I asked her why she had continued the patrols, she replied, 'I wanted that so-and-so in prison.'

Two good police officers both doing their duty to put dangerous men behind bars, but there unfortunately the similarity ends. WPC Parrott and her female companion were both awarded George Medals and the arrest was carried out by a holder of the George Cross.[2] There would be no medals for Finch. 'The whole incident changed my life, completely,' he told me. 'There hasn't been one day go by without me thinking about the event.'

It was Lester Purdy who some thirty years after the incident mentioned a number of theories to me. One was that someone was wearing the black wig in the car to pretend that they were Sue Stephens, so that she could slip away to meet Martin. Really,

---

2. For a fuller version of this heroic event, see the author's book *The Brave Blue Line* (Wharncliffe Books, 2011).

this is nonsense. Both Purdy and Peter Enter had put the wig on as a joke, the latter at Stephens's address on 14 January. Stephens had suggested he wear it for a dare in the street and he did; he kept it on until the others got into the Mini, when Stephens snatched it off him and threw it into the Mini and there it remained. 'I think that theory was made up by the police to make us look bad because it fooled them into attempted murder,' Purdy told me. Well, this was a new one to me. The fact remains that the wig was used, but only by Stephens when she had previously met Martin.

The next of Purdy's rumours was that it had been suggested they had deliberately set out to decoy the police, to make them believe that Martin was in the Mini; however, he added, 'what would have been the purpose of that?' Purdy was quite right; to decoy the police away from what? If that had been the case, the police would have had to have believed that Martin was in a certain place, at a certain time, as would the occupants of the Mini in order to draw the police away from him, but this was simply not the case. The car's occupants correctly said they were going to Coulsdon to pick up a car for a film shoot. The Mini was hired in Purdy's name and paid for with a cheque drawn from his account, not the sort of behaviour one associates with conspirators.

Neil Dickens agreed. 'These speculations are totally wrong,' he said. 'The tragedy of this whole sad affair was the genuine mistaken identity of Waldorf.' Steve Holloway concurred. 'Personally, I think they were just going about their daily business,' he told me. 'Like you, I can't see any credence in a decoy theory. I'd be surprised if they were actually capable of thinking that way and I can't see a reason to do so.'

So that's the theory of them being a decoy dispensed with, but nonetheless their behaviour in the car was certain to draw attention to them. At the car hire company, DC Robert Bruce saw Waldorf, who at that time was standing on the pavement outside the company, 'go to the Capri and leaned in to the rear of the vehicle and took what appeared to be a briefcase and brolly from the rear'. During his interview (and referring to the yellow Mini), DC Deane said, 'I saw that Purdy was driving, the unknown man [Waldorf] ... was sitting in the front passenger seat and he was motioning towards Susan Stephens who was in the rear seat, to keep lying down'. DC Cyril Jenner said, '... it had been observed that the front seat passenger kept going down as if delving into a case or bag, but this was some time prior to the shooting'.

And during his interview with Commander Taylor, Jardine said, 'I think it's probably relevant to say at this point that on the approach to the Shepherd's Bush roundabout, DC Deane and I noticed that Susie kept ducking or lying down on the back seat. We also saw the front passenger from time to time was leaning over to the back seat and opening or tampering with a briefcase and some packages. DC Deane and I discussed between ourselves the possibility that Susie was either trying to avoid surveillance or had been told to keep her head down in case some trouble started.'

Even David Still, the passenger in the Volkswagen van behind the yellow Mini in Pembroke Road, stated, 'I also noticed a girl in the back of the Mini who had been sitting up and looking out of the back window and then lying down out of sight. She appeared to do this, several times.'

This odd behaviour was unravelled by Lester Purdy. He explained to me that he had been part of a group of Second World War fanatics who bought up a number of ex-wartime vehicles and carried out manoeuvres, mainly in Wales, using large fireworks which they set off at ground level. 'We were on pot and LSD,' he told me, 'so it was real to us.' One morning after a party,

Purdy's address was visited by two men, whom he described as being 'Special Branch, and armed'. A lot of the guests were still there. The officers questioned him about the manoeuvres and the explosions and asked if he had any political affiliations but Purdy gave them a truthful explanation as to the activities, which they accepted. 'They could of easily busted us all for pot, etc., they saw it and joked about it, then left,' said Purdy.

However, Purdy thought that the Special Branch officers might tip off the Drugs Squad and this appeared to be confirmed a few days before the shooting when he, Stephens and a friend were driving in the King's Road, Chelsea. He felt they were being followed, but as he told me, 'I didn't try to lose them, just made them aware we knew; I had nothing to hide, anyway.'

But on 14 January there was something to hide. When Purdy and co. left West End Lane in his Capri, he did not believe he was being followed and after transferring to the Mini, his mood of optimism continued because as Purdy told me, 'I must have been at ease because pretty much every red light we stopped at we all had a snort, Steve was chopping up lines on my briefcase and we were passing it back and forth, which is what we were doing in Pembroke Road.'

The behaviour in the Mini does tend to confirm that witnessed by the police and civilian witnesses but what did the occupants of the Mini have to say about it? The answer is, differing versions.

Purdy was being fairly ambiguous when he told Neil Dickens, and also his solicitor Arwyn Hopkins, 'Prior to leaving the flat at West End Lane on the Friday, I didn't take any drugs and I didn't see anyone else take any. But when I got home, I took some drugs because I was shocked.'

Susan Stephens was slightly less disingenuous. Telling the investigating officers that she laid down in the Mini, she suggested a contributory factor to her weariness may have been, as she later told a newspaper, 'The night before, I had been to an all-night video party: *E.T.*, *The Poltergeist* and lots of pot.' Referring to the day of the shooting, she said, 'Yesterday, I took a small amount of drugs. I had a line of heroin and cocaine, mixed,' although she stated that this was prior to getting into the Mini. In a further statement made to Detective Chief Inspector Siddle in the presence of her solicitor, Michael Caplan, and referring to Waldorf, she added, 'Steven is not an addict but he does take heroin, occasionally. I have no knowledge if he took heroin that day. Lester Purdy also takes heroin but I have no knowledge whether he took any that day or had any in his possession.' Upon their arrival at the hospital and referring to Waldorf, Jane Lamprill heard her say, 'Be careful what drugs you give him, he's on heroin,' and Stephens agreed in essence with that statement. This was taken on board by Dr Peter Opie at St Stephen's who in treating Waldorf carried out '… tests for the presence of the Hepatitis B Surface and Antigen, as we heard that the accompanying female was a known hepatitis risk'.

What did Steven Waldorf say? Probably the frankest of them all, he told Neil Dickens, 'I have been asked if I heard Susie say anything about my having taken heroin. I have in the past experimented by smoking heroin but when I have taken drugs more recently, it has been cocaine. I would like to add here that having experimented, I am now against them. I do not consider myself to be an addict in any way.' However, he added, 'When we were in the Mini that evening, some time before we arrived in the traffic jam where I was shot, I had taken a line of cocaine. That means sniffing a small amount up my nose.'

The last of Purdy's theories is that when he ran from the car, it was said that he was in possession of a gun. Telling me, 'The gun theory also doesn't make sense; I ran for my life', and I could find no one who disagreed with him. 'I would have thought that most people would try to save themselves when being involved in such a firearms incident,' said Neil Dickens and as Steve Holloway with characteristic bluntness told me, 'he was saving his own arse.'

But Purdy persisted that the police had put this rumour about. 'The police knew I didn't have a gun and it was very convenient that I got away; it meant anything could be said,' he told me. 'I was in the wrong place at the wrong time – surely you realise that?'

As a matter of fact, I do.

Blame was freely apportioned and responsibility abdicated. Martin agreed that he had shot PC Carr but added as a corollary, 'it is his fault for actually grabbing my hand and wrenching my arm about.' Martin's father, blithely disregarding his son's chequered criminal history, claimed that his conviction and sentence had come about because 'he had taken the can back for the Waldorf shooting'. Following her daughter's conviction, Mrs Patricia Stephens said, 'My daughter is being victimised for being a friend of David Martin.' Sir Ivan Lawrence appeared to blame the prison officers for not earlier finding the flex with which Martin hanged himself. Only in the case of Jardine and Finch did they say, in effect, 'Yes, we did it, we made a terrible mistake and we're sorry.'

But when all was said and done, as one officer who was marginally involved in the case told me with masterly under-statement, 'It was not the Met's finest hour.'

He was right; it wasn't.

Epilogue

Over forty years ago, I knew a detective who had a pre-occupation with his looks, an overpowering arrogance and an unshakeable belief in his sexual attractiveness. He was a prolific womaniser although an indiscriminate one; on three occasions his dalliances resulted in him being infected with a dose of the clap. As well as nervously avoiding the lavatory seat in the cubicle which he had recently vacated in the washroom, the rest of us grew mightily fed up with the way in which he admired his reflection. We mere mortals would simply glance in the washroom's mirror to check that our hair was neatly combed; he preened himself for what seemed like hours in front of it. At last, I could tolerate this state of affairs no longer. 'Tell me, John,' I said (while ensuring that a crowd as large as possible was present). 'If you could live your life all over again, would you still fall in love with yourself?'

This brings us to David Martin, who you may agree was not dissimilar in several respects to 'John'. No doubt, I shall be asked by the media in the years to come 'Didn't you have a sneaking regard for Martin?' The answer is not something I shall have to ruminate about for too long; the answer will be a flat, unequivocal 'No'. I did not hold him in any kind of regard at all, sneaking or otherwise. I described Martin at Knightsbridge Crown Court as being 'the most dangerous man in London' and although over thirty years have passed since then, I still adhere to my description of David Ralph Martin. Before and after that investigation, I met criminals who were tougher and more violent plus some who, like Martin, had no redeeming features whatsoever, but for sheer professionalism, coolness, resolution and ruthlessness, Martin reigned supreme. As far as I was concerned, Martin was a near-psychotic, out-of-control, manipulative, murderous piece of garbage. Harsh words? Yes, I agree but I happen to think they're the most appropriate ones.

Even if one were to accept – which I most conspicuously do not – his denial in court that it was not he who pulled the trigger when security guard Edward Burns was shot, he was part of that cold-blooded robbery and in possession of one of the stolen guns. There was no denying that he certainly pulled the trigger – three times – when confronted by Police Constable Carr whom he shot one week later; and it was not his fault that PC Carr did not die from his injuries. And six weeks after that, I am under no illusions whatsoever that if he had been given the opportunity to use either of the fully loaded handguns in his possession when he was arrested by DC Peter Finch and PC Steve Lucas, he would have done so, with murderous intent.

Was there any truth in Martin's assertions in court that he wished to acquire firearms in order to kill himself, in the event that he was threatened with capture? No, in my opinion, none at all. I believe that at the moment of his arrest, he wanted the police to shoot him, hence walking towards them refusing to raise his hands. Had that occurred, in his twisted psyche, he would have achieved iconic status, since he would have engineered his own death. And looking at matters from a common-sense point of view, why would anyone go to all the trouble – while being London's No. 1 wanted man – to break into an office, to get details of people who wanted to sell guns and go and photograph the exterior of their home addresses, presumably prior to breaking in and stealing the firearms, simply to commit suicide? The whole concept is ludicrous; especially when you consider there are far easier ways of committing suicide, as Martin found out.

I accept that at the time of Martin's arrest in the Underground tunnel, he was not in possession of a firearm, nor did he have access to one. If he had, I have no doubt that he would have opened fire at his pursuers and would have killed or incapacitated as many of them as possible before, once more, attempting to escape.

Martin was brilliant, certainly, in his knowledge and expertise when dealing with locks and security devices, but since he utilised that knowledge to commit offences, instead of strengthening the weaknesses he found in those security systems – which as I have already suggested would have made him his fortune by the security companies – is that something to be admired? Not by me, although with the values which are held nowadays by many members of the public as to where wrong is right and vice versa, I should think that my opinion is only held by a minority. And yet, ironically, Martin described himself as a security expert, a security advisor. At his trial, Martin told the jury that in late 1982, he had been involved in security work, adding that he had 'reasonable ability' in his field, including the ability to enter buildings. And while the Flying Squad was still hunting him, Martin's friend Philip Lee told the press that he had seen him several times during the summer of 1982. 'He told me his job was selling bugging equipment and he used to go out of town now and then, supposedly to see business clients,' said Lee. 'His flat was filled with gadgetry and he never stopped talking about it. He even asked me to make him some sort of bugging device once but he was a bit of a rambler. He used to go on and on and on.'

'He was,' added Lee, 'a bit of a dreamer.' Not, however, according to former Detective Sergeant Roger Clements. 'Out of all the criminals I ever dealt with, there were only two that I regarded as being pure evil,' he told me. 'One was an IRA quartermaster and the other was David Martin.' Martin was rotten through and through. He chose his lifestyle, nobody else. He did not have to become a criminal and the fact that he did, was his choice. I heard that when Martin was told that Steven Waldorf had been shot by police, he wept; call me Old Mr Cynical if you like but if he did, I should think they were tears of laughter. Controlling and cunning, it seemed as though his criminal acts were just one long dare, to 'catch me if you can'. And when he was caught, whatever he had done was always somebody else's fault.

As for the escape from the cells at Marlborough Street Magistrates' Court, it was a widely held belief that he had used a metal spoon or perhaps a plastic knife to pick the lock of the cell door, except that on the inside of a cell door there is no lock to pick, just a flat steel plate. Nor did he use a duplicate key, for precisely the same reason. The answer is far more simple. As I mentioned previously, during the large number of journeys he made to the cells at court, his meek and mild manner lulled his captors into a false sense of security. It was Mick Geraghty who unravelled this conundrum as he chatted to Martin when he took his fingerprints; let him tell the story:

> He noticed that the jailer only pushed the cell door closed and did not secure it further. Martin obtained a sheet of Perspex in prison and when he attended the court and the cell door was closed, he slipped the sheet between the door and the door jamb to prevent the lock sliding home. At an appropriate time, he had only to push the cell door open and having worked out the route, walked out of the cells and out of the building. He said that he did not say how in his interviews, as he did not want to get the jailer into trouble.

And there is one matter that all of us should remember: directly or indirectly, David Martin was responsible for injuries and/ or trauma to quite a number of people and their families who feature in this book. This caveat also applies to any liberal-minded council who might, one day, be induced to put up a blue plaque to him, perhaps at the slum in Finsbury Park where he grew up, maybe at the stinking dump at Notting Hill where he spent his last few hours of freedom or else Hampstead Underground station. Mind you, I think Martin would have loved that.

As he once said to a friend, 'If you've got the bottle, you can make the world dance for you.' And perhaps for a short time in London during the early 1980s, it did.

Bibliography

Ball, John, Chester, Lewis & Perrott, Roy, *Cops and Robbers*, Andre Deutsch, London, 1978.

Cater, Frank with Tullett, Tom, *The Sharp End*, The Bodley Head, London, 1988.

Fido, Martin and Skinner, Keith, *The Official Encyclopedia of Scotland Yard*, Virgin Books, London, 1999.

Gosling, John with Tullett, Tom, *The Ghost Squad*, W.H. Allen, London, 1959.

Graham, Winston, *Great Cases of Scotland Yard, Volume Two: 'The Wembley Job'*, The Reader's Digest Association Ltd, London, 1978.

Kelland, Gilbert, *Crime in London*, HarperCollins, London, 1993.

Kirby, Dick, *Rough Justice*, Merlin Unwin Books, Ludlow, 2001.

Kirby, Dick, *The Sweeney*, Wharncliffe Books, Barnsley, 2011.

Kirby, Dick, *The Brave Blue Line*, Wharncliffe Books, Barnsley, 2011.

Kirby, Dick, *Death on the Beat*, Wharncliffe Books, Barnsley, 2012.

Lawrence, Sir Ivan, *My Life of Crime – Cases & Causes*, Book Guild Publishing, Kibworth, 2010.

Mark, Sir Robert, *In the Office of Constable*, Collins, London, 1978.

Parker, Norman, *Dangerous People, Dangerous Places*, John Blake Publishing, London, 2007.

Read, Leonard with Morton, James, *Nipper*, Macdonald & Co.,
    London, 1991.
Real Life Crimes ... And How They Were Solved, Issue 38,
    Eaglemoss Productions, 1993.
Roach, Eddie, 'A Crime Revisited', unpublished document.
Rubin, Gareth, *The Great Cat Massacre – A History of Britain in
    100 Mistakes*, John Blake Publishing, London, 2014.
Waldren, Michael J., *Armed Police*, Sutton Publishing, Stroud,
    2007.

About the Author

Dick Kirby was born in the East End of London and joined the Metropolitan Police in 1967. Half of his twenty-six years' service was spent with Scotland Yard's Serious Crime Squad and the Flying Squad.

Kirby contributes to newspapers and magazines, as well as appearing on television and the radio. This is his twelfth true crime book and in his retirement he lives with his family near Bury St Edmunds, Suffolk. He can be visited at his website: www.dickkirby.com

Index